UNDERSTANDING
WILLIAM T. VOLLMANN

UNDERSTANDING CONTEMPORARY AMERICAN LITERATURE

Matthew J. Bruccoli, Founding Editor

Linda Wagner-Martin, Series Editor

Also of Interest

Understanding Chuck Palahniuk, by Douglas Keesey

Understanding Francisco Goldman, by Ariana E. Vigil

Understanding Gerald Vizenor, by Deborah L. Madsen

Understanding Dave Eggers, by Timothy W. Galow

Understanding Graham Swift, by David Malcolm

Understanding Jim Grimsley, by David Deutsch

Understanding John Irving, by Edward C. Reilly

Understanding Jonathan Lethem, by Matthew Luter

Understanding Nelson Algren, by Brooke Horvath

Understanding Ron Rash, by John Lang

UNDERSTANDING

WILLIAM T. VOLLMANN

Işıl Özcan

THE UNIVERSITY OF
SOUTH CAROLINA PRESS

Published by the University of South Carolina Press
Columbia, South Carolina 29208

www.sc.edu/uscpress

Manufactured in the United States of America

28 27 26 25 24 23 22 21 20 19
10 9 8 7 6 5 4 3 2 1

Library of Congress Cataloging-in-Publication Data
can be found at http://catalog.loc.gov/.

ISBN 978-1-64336-029-4 (hardback)

For Jonathan Arac

CONTENTS

SERIES EDITOR'S PREFACE

The Understanding Contemporary American Literature series was founded by the estimable Matthew J. Bruccoli (1931–2008), who envisioned these volumes as guides or companions for students as well as good nonacademic readers, a legacy that will continue as new volumes are developed to fill in gaps among the nearly one hundred series volumes published to date and to embrace a host of new writers only now making their marks on our literature.

As Professor Bruccoli explained in his preface to the volumes he edited, because much influential contemporary literature makes special demands, "the word *understanding* in the titles was chosen deliberately. Many willing readers lack an adequate understanding of how contemporary literature works; that is, of what the author is attempting to express and the means by which it is conveyed." Aimed at fostering this understanding of good literature and good writers, the criticism and analysis in the series provide instruction in how to read certain contemporary writers—explicating their material, language, structures, themes, and perspectives—and facilitate a more profitable experience of the works under discussion.

In the twenty-first century Professor Bruccoli's prescience gives us an avenue to publish expert critiques of significant contemporary American writing. The series continues to map the literary landscape and to provide both instruction and enjoyment. Future volumes will seek to introduce new voices alongside canonized favorites, to chronicle the changing literature of our times, and to remain, as Professor Bruccoli conceived, contemporary in the best sense of the word.

Linda Wagner-Martin, Series Editor

ACKNOWLEDGMENTS

I would like to thank University of Pittsburgh for granting me a postdoctoral fellowship (2015–17) to work on this project. I am most grateful to my mentor, Jonathan Arac, for his guidance, advice, and generosity.

Permission to use material from Vollmann's works is gratefully acknowledged:

Excerpt(s) from *Whores for Gloria* by William T. Vollmann, © 1991 by William T. Vollmann. Reproduced with permission of the Licensor through PLSclear.

From *William T. Vollmann: A Critical Study and Seven Interviews* © 2009 Michael Hemmingson by permission of McFarland & Company, Inc., Box 611, Jefferson NC 28640. www.mcfarlandbooks.com.

Brief quotations from pp. 1, 2, 28, 33, 87, 88, 225, 244 from *Kissing the Mask* by William T. Vollmann. © 2010 by William Vollmann. Reprinted by permission of HarperCollins Publishers.

Numerous brief quotations: pp. xi – 663 [1857 words] from *Rising Up and Rising Down* by William T. Vollmann. © 2004 by William T. Vollmann. Reprinted by permission of HarperCollins Publishers.

Brief quotations from pp. xii, xiv, xv, xxi, 8, 16, 101, 130, 170, 238, 239, 263, 271, 283 from *Poor People* by William T. Vollmann. © 2007 by William T. Vollmann. Reprinted by permission of HarperCollins Publishers.

Excerpt(s) from *The Ice-Shirt: Volume One of Seven Dreams: a Book of North American Landscapes* by William T. Vollmann, © 1990 by William T. Vollmann. Used by permission of Viking Books, an imprint of Penguin Publishing Group, a division of Penguin Random House LLC. All rights reserved.

Excerpt(s) from *The Rifles: Volume Six of Seven Dreams: a Book of North American Landscapes* by William T. Vollmann, © 1994 by William T. Vollmann. Used by permission of Viking Books, an imprint of Penguin Publishing Group, a division of Penguin Random House LLC. All rights reserved.

Excerpt(s) from *The Atlas* by William T. Vollmann, © 1996 by William T. Vollmann. Used by permission of Viking Books, an imprint of Penguin Publishing Group, a division of Penguin Random House LLC. All rights reserved.

Text from sources listed below reprinted by permission of Writers House LLC, acting as agent for the author:

The Ice-Shirt: Volume One of Seven Dreams: A Book of North American Landscapes. UK & Commonwealth (incl. Canada) distribution rights for hardcover. Publisher: Penguin Books. © William T Vollmann, 1990.

The Rifles: Volume Six Of Seven Dreams: A Book of North American Landscapes (790 words). UK & Commonwealth (incl. Canada) distribution rights for hardcover. Publisher: Penguin Books. © William T. Vollmann, 1994.

Europe Central. UK & Commonwealth (excl. Canada) distribution rights for hardcover. Publisher: Viking. © William T. Vollmann, 2005.

Imperial. UK & Commonwealth (excl. Canada) distribution rights for hardcover. Publisher: Viking. © William T. Vollmann, 2009.

The Dying Grass: A Novel of The Nez Perce War. UK & Commonwealth (excl. Canada) distribution rights for hardcover. Publisher: Viking. © 2015 by William T. Vollmann.

Kissing the Mask. UK & Commonwealth (excl. Canada) Distribution rights for hardcover. Publisher: Ecco. © William T. Vollmann, 2010.

Poor People. UK & Commonwealth (excl. Canada) Distribution rights for hardcover. Publisher: Ecco. © 2007 by William T. Vollmann.

Expelled from Eden: A William T. Vollmann Reader. Publisher: Thunder's Mouth Press. © 2004 by Larry McCaffery and Michael Hemmingson.

The Book of Dolores. Publisher: powerHouse Books. © 2013 by William T. Vollmann.

Butterfly Stories. Publisher: The Grove Press. © 1993 by William T. Vollmann.

An Afghanistan Picture Show. Publisher: Farrar, Straus & Giroux. © 1992 by William T. Vollmann.

Foreword to Jackson Newell's *The Electric Edge of Academe. The Saga of Lucien L. Nunn and Deep Springs College*. Publisher: University of Utah Press. Foreword © 2015 by William T. Vollmann.

Afterword to Danilo Kiš's *A Tomb for Boris Davidovich* (18 words). Publisher: Dalkey Archive. Afterword © 2001 by William T. Vollmann.

Afterword to Bernard Wolfe's *The Great Prince Died*. Publisher: University of Chicago Press. Afterword © 2015 by William T. Vollmann.

Afterword to Heinrich Böll's novella *The Train Was on Time*. Publisher: Melville House. Afterword © 2011 by William T. Vollmann.

CHAPTER 1

Understanding William T. Vollmann

William Tanner Vollmann was born on July 28, 1959, in Santa Monica, California, to Thomas E. Vollmann and Tanis Vollmann. After his father completed his PhD in business at UCLA, he started teaching at Dartmouth College, and the family moved to New Hampshire. Vollmann was a bookish, solitary child, reading mostly science fiction. He wrote a novel before he was ten years old, which (naturally) was a work of science fiction about astronauts and their unsuccessful space adventures. When Vollmann was nine years old, his six-year-old sister, Julie, drowned in a pond while she was left in Vollmann's care—a tragedy that has always haunted Vollmann. The family moved to Providence, Rhode Island, and then to Bloomington, Indiana, as Vollmann's father accepted new faculty positions. In 1977, Vollmann finished high school in Bloomington and enrolled at Deep Springs College, an all-male college located on a cattle ranch in the desert of California. Deep Springs champions an "educational program on democratic self-governance, personal responsibility, and study of the liberal arts and sciences—all designed to instill an ethic of service to humanity" (Newell xiv). The students are expected to excel not only in courses such as applied philosophy, thermodynamics, and world history but also in the physical requirements of maintaining the ranch and community, from irrigation and slaughter to cooking and cleaning. In other words, "farm and ranch labor rival academic demands for students' time" (Newell xv). In his foreword to L. Jackson Newell's *The Electric Edge of Academe. The Saga of Lucien L. Nunn and Deep Springs College,* Vollmann notes that he arrived at Deep Springs "in dread of physical labor" but it "taught me to prepare for a life of service" (xii). Deep Springs "taught me to go and see things for myself, to get the best information about problems I could, to worry a lot and plan a lot, until the unfamiliar became comprehensible, and only then (crossing my fingers and hoping for the best) to *do* my best" (*Expelled from Eden*, 33).

Vollmann enrolled at Cornell University in 1979. He stayed at the Telluride House and graduated from the comparative literature program summa cum laude in 1981. Next, he won a fellowship from the graduate program in literature at University of California, Berkeley, which he deferred because he was so bewildered by what he considered an obvious case of good versus evil: the Soviets had invaded Afghanistan. Vollmann decided to fight along with the Afghan mujahideen against the invasion.[1] He was broke, so he first saved money working as a coffee-serving, jacket-holding secretary in a reinsurance company. He arrived in Afghanistan in 1982 only to get miserably sick with dysentery and came back home much sooner than he had planned. He did not accomplish any of his goals on this adventure, yet the material he collected from that failed trip evolved into *An Afghanistan Picture Show* (1992) and provided the seed of his life's work that would take two decades to complete, *Rising Up and Rising Down* (2003).

Writing appealed more than academic studies to Vollmann, so he left the graduate program, moved to San Francisco, and worked at further odd jobs to make a living, including as a door-to-door canvasser and, through a friend's help, a computer programmer. He knew nothing about programming, but the latter job gave him access to a computer on which he could write. Vollmann worked on his first novel *You Bright and Risen Angels* (1987) during off hours in a Silicon Valley office, living on snack bars and soda from the vending machine, and curling up to sleep under the desk behind a wastebasket to camouflage himself from the cleaners. *You Bright and Risen Angels* is a science fictional parable about revolutionaries who themselves become oppressors in which bugs and insects enter into battle with electricity. When it was published, it brought him critical acclaim and a Whiting Writers Award and alerted critics of contemporary literature of his arrival. Tom LeClair informed Larry McCaffery of Vollmann, and McCaffery became the first—and has remained the foremost—Vollmann scholar, introducing Vollmann to pretty much all of us. Perhaps the most important episode in Vollmann's San Francisco years was his meeting with one of the most important figures in the development of his aesthetic sensibility: the photographer and aficionado of street life Ken Miller. Miller introduced Vollmann to San Francisco's red-light zones, and while Miller photographed skinheads, prostitutes, and other people from the margins, Vollmann decided to write about them, which got his creative juices flowing. *The Rainbow Stories* (1989), part documentary, part fictional outcome of Vollmann's time with people Miller photographed, was followed by *Whores for Gloria* (1991), a story about a lovelorn Vietnam veteran's search for his girlfriend among prostitutes in the Tenderloin district of San Francisco, *Thirteen Stories and Thirteen Epitaphs* (1992), stories in the vein of *The Rainbow Stories,* and the semiautobiographical *Butterfly Stories* (1993) narrating Vollmann and Miller's decadent experiences throughout their travels in Asia.

Vollmann became aware of completely new modes of existence during his time in San Francisco. Perhaps more importantly, he realized how little he knew about America. While writing *The Rainbow Stories,* he decided he needed to understand America in all its complexity and began planning a project that would become the novel cycle that narrates a symbolic history of America, Seven Dreams: A Book of North American Landscapes. Starting with the first Americans, the native populations of North America, and its first colonizers, the Greenlanders, Vollmann reimagines the history of conflicts and collisions between cultures in seven novels modeled after Ovid's *Metamorphoses* to chart the successive ages of the continent. He has so far published five novels from the cycle in the order he completed manuscripts rather than in a chronological order of the sequence: *The Ice-Shirt: First Dream* (1990), *Fathers and Crows: Second Dream* (1992), *The Rifles: Sixth Dream* (1994), *Argall: The True Story of Pocahontas and Captain John Smith: Third Dream* (2001), and *The Dying Grass: Fifth Dream* (2015).

In the 1990s, Vollmann began writing for magazines and journals and has since been traveling around the world on commission from publications such as *Spin, Gear, Esquire,* the *New Yorker,* and the *Los Angeles Times.* He reports mostly from sites of danger and war: Somalia, Burma, Sarajevo, Iraq, Iran, Kosovo, Cambodia, and Fukushima, Japan are some places he has visited. Being on journalistic errands has enabled Vollmann to carry out research on personal projects that forms the backbone of most of his books, not to mention that it has brought him some financial stability. Perhaps the only instance Vollmann allows editorial intervention to his writing would be these pieces because Vollmann is otherwise notorious for refusing changes to his books, whether to their length or their punctuation. As far as content is concerned, there is considerable discrepancy between the magazine versions of his pieces and their extended, uncut, unedited versions in Vollmann's books.[2] His magazine and journal writing qualifies as feature writing rather than conventional journalism. Vollmann's journalism, like that of Hemingway, whom Vollmann admires, is highly subjective and participative. We get the sense that Vollmann does not consider working simultaneously on fiction (broadly defined here to include works like *An Afghanistan Picture Show* as well as his war correspondence) and nonfiction as a circumstance that poses a conflict. Both genres are compatible with the means and ends of his writing. Vollmann does not proceed as if there is a distinction between being a fiction writer and being a nonfiction writer but instead aims at accurate representation of subjects in which he feels personally invested. Furthermore, there is a strong sense of correspondence between his fiction and nonfiction, when, for example, a strain of research on a particular topic yields enough material and generates substantial insight to be presented in both fiction and nonfiction without overlapping, as we see in the case of his unpublished novel *How You Are* about a Mexican transgender sex worker and his takes on performative aspects of gender and femininity in *Kissing the Mask* and *The Book of Dolores.* Of course it does not mean that research always guarantees enough insight to write a novel, as Vollmann's research on the US-Mexico border proves: he has abandoned the initial plan for a novel because he had decided to present his research in its full complexity in the nonfictional format in *Imperial,* which he calls his *Moby-Dick.*

To date, he has about forty books to his name, including fiction, nonfiction, books of photography and handmade book objects, and a number of awards including the National Book Award, Strauss Living Award, the PEN / Hemingway Award, and two listings as a finalist for the National Book Critics Circle Award. Vollmann's writing displays the presence of a world historian, ethnographer, moral philosopher, and investigative journalist. Uncontainable to any single genre, his work combines fiction, nonfiction, memoir, the essay, journalism, war correspondence, social and cultural critique, philosophical treatise, political theory, ecocriticism, and history. He has published many handmade book objects with CoTangent Press, which he founded. He is also a successful visual artist, and his drawings, paintings, and photography frequently appear in his books and in art galleries. Recent editions of American literature anthologies include his work, and since 1992, the Ohio State University has been archiving his material.

Vollmann is an insatiable reader besides being a prolific writer. Any analysis of Vollmann has to consider his ferocious reading of and exceptionally wide range of knowledge in world literature. He is a *man of letters* in the traditional sense of the term. He is well learned in world literature, history, and philosophy. His literary affinities and literary influences lie as much with American traditions as with European and Asian literature. His favorite writers include Nathaniel Hawthorne, Herman Melville, Walt Whitman, Edgar Allan Poe, James Agee, Ernest Hemingway, John Steinbeck, Yasunari Kawabata, Murasaki Shikibu, Comte de Lautréamont, Leo Tolstoy, and Danilo Kiš. To talk about the works that have shaped Vollmann's literary sensibility as his "influences" would be to understate the case because most of them have had life-changing influences on him, such as *A Tomb for Boris Davidovich* by Kiš, *Let Us Now Praise Famous Men* by James Agee and Walker Evans, *Palm-of-the-Hand Stories* by Kawabata, and *East of Eden* by Steinbeck. Vollmann acknowledges his debt to these authors throughout his works, which often structure themselves as conversations with these masters. In the many afterwords he has written to reprints of his favorite novels, as well as in his afterwords to Danilo Kiš's *A Tomb for Boris Davidovich*, George Simenon's *Dirty Snow*, Bernard Wolfe's *The Great Prince Died: A Novel about the Assassination of Trotsky*, and Malcolm Lowry's *Under the Volcano*, Vollmann expresses his appreciation of these authors. He also has written reviews of the works of Guy Davenport, Robert Coover, W. G. Sebald, and Anthony Swifford.

It is not rare for major novelists to receive belated, at times posthumous, recognition. The category of the "literary revival" denotes such debts of appreciation. Maybe no revival can be as groundbreaking as the so-called Melville revival of the 1920s, which began in England and spread to the United States in waves. Similarly, the swelling of interest in Faulkner in the 1940s, which divided his ongoing career radically into two periods, brought him not only recognition but a Nobel Prize. A similar moment may be near at hand in contemporary letters. William T. Vollmann, whose assurance that he will win the Nobel Prize one day seems more and more likely with every new volume he publishes, has begun to receive growing appreciation after a considerable time of neglect. This is not to say that Vollmann has toiled in oblivion, but it seems that potential readers require more encouragement to start reading his books, which look intimidating, long, and difficult—postmodern, if you will. The aura of difficulty and the intimidating bulkiness of his output has definitely limited the level of appreciation of his works, not to mention his unbeatable publication rate that brings out one maximalist tome after another. However, the dazzlingly prolific Vollmann is a contemporary cataloguer of epic proportions in the vein of Walt Whitman and Herman Melville rather than being a member of the cohort of postmodern novelists. If there is anything strictly postmodern about his work, it derives from the political and avant-garde thrust of the 1960s and 1970s.[3] Furthermore, he does not write like Thomas Pynchon, contrary to what has commonly been claimed.[4] It would be more accurate to see in him Whitman's expanding and contracting self, Poe's obsession with guilt and sin, Hawthorne's love for the parable, and Steinbeck's sympathy for the wretched, Hemingway's thirst and the courage he showed as a witness to conflict and in reporting on it. Also questionable are the (non)critical commonplaces about his work being all about his experiences with street people. Vollmann writes more about ethics, violence, history, war, love, and death than he does about his encounters with sex workers and the occasional crack he has smoked with them. In Vollmann's case, the abundance of biographical elements of his work seem to have prevented a full-scale reception of his work. This is not to say that biographical aspects of his work do not help our understanding of him.

On the contrary, many psychological undercurrents and the arc of his career may be illuminated by looking at his life without one having to resort to the cult of personality. After all, his deep knowledge of world history and world literature and the rare interest he shows in world politics are the driving force of his works as much as his experiences in red-light zones around the globe. As Daniel Lukes notes, "part of the problem is that when he writes about prostitution, Vollmann . . . does not write about it from a distance but as a 'john' himself'" (248). It seems to be the case that the autobiographical strain in his writing fuels sensationalism, and it has been emphasized at the cost of critical attention to his work.

Vollmann's work proves strikingly relevant to current discussions in the humanities. He has been exploring in theory and illustrating in practice some issues that keep scholars and thinkers busy. The humanities have been questioning their role in public life, their institutional legitimacy and influence, the significance of their moral guidance, and their political effect, as well as their future in the face of technological and digital revolutions for some time now. Since the late 1980s, Vollmann has been asking what humanistic inquiry and literature can do for the world and humanity. Without a doubt, his commitment to the political, the historical, and the ethical helps turn his literary program into an ongoing humanities project. More specifically, his work displays surprising solidarity with the contemporary disciplinary concerns of American literary studies, which has been trying to define new relationships among culture, nation, and world in the last two decades. Literary scholars agree that the nation and the literary field do not legitimize each other anymore. There are efforts to integrate American literature and comparative literary studies, which is itself being redefined through amalgamations with world literature and area studies. The status of the nation as a literary paradigm continues to remain controversial. The question is how best to define a modified, that is, denationalized, globalized, hemispheric, transnational American literature. Indeed, what are the implications of these modifications of "the American"?

Vollmann's work illuminates such concerns. He is highly aware of the fallacies of the "nation" paradigm. As Christopher Coffman notes, "given his oft-expressed interest in foreign literatures, a view of Vollmann as participating in a narrowly defined national tradition would be misrepresentative" ("Feverish Fictions," 246). He writes both about American and non-American issues without treating either as determining his identity as a writer. He wants to understand how human life unfolds in different geographies, and his compassionate interest is not bounded by territorial units. He writes as passionately and in depth about the US-Mexico border as about the visible and invisible borders created by ethnicity in the former Yugoslavia. In telling the unknown stories of the downtrodden, the socially and politically repressed, the marginalized and stigmatized, Vollmann gives voice to the extraterritorial, excluded, and silenced. Vollmann extends his empathy across the planet by refusing to distinguish people he knows and cares about from those he does not, an approach captured by Gayatri Spivak with her notion of planetarity. He takes it as his natural calling to write about the world; his national identity does not determine his subject matter. He opens American literature to the world with the conviction that the planet poses the ultimate ethical challenge.

There is little that Vollmann has written about and not personally experienced himself. For many readers, the scope and the force of Vollmann's openness to the other is inseparable from his method and conduct. The name of a Facebook fan group, "What Would William Tanner Vollmann Do?" encapsulates the fascination with the ways in which Vollmann delves into circumstances in order to uncover the stories underneath them. He is distinctive for his ability to write without objectifying others. In his extensive travels and interviews around the world, he seeks firsthand experience about the lives of the people he writes about. In the scenes he sets up that detail interaction with others, he analyzes, but perhaps more importantly, he puts himself at stake. Physical harm comes with the territory: in the course of his research, he got dysentery in Afghanistan and frostbite in the North Pole, was caught in a mine explosion in Bosnia, rafted on poisonous rivers in California, and was exposed to radioactivity in the Fukushima nuclear disaster zone. Vollmann puts himself at stake emotionally as well. Rendering himself vulnerable helps him connect with others, earn their trust, and come to know them so that he can write more realistically and truthfully about them. Vollmann seeks truth in difficult situations not with the assurance that he is safe and immune but with the realization that the other's truth will change his own outlook, his own life, and consequently, ours. Mostly, that truth amounts to life-threatening violence, despair, poverty, pain, and helplessness. For him, "when people are in extreme situations, somehow their innate character, their essence is X-rayed by the blinding rays of horror" (Goldberg, n.p.). Subjecting himself to those rays of horror along with those people, Vollmann recounts and stages encounters with the other; each ethically intimate encounter takes the form of an existential risk, and he invites the reader to search for truth, human integrity and beauty, and redemption along with him.

Vollmann attends to the world, and the world has paid attention. This fact distinguishes Vollmann from his contemporaries and many of his predecessors. Sparking interest not only in the United States both also in Europe, Vollmann's works have inspired critics and scholars to chart the contours of contemporary fiction, develop new theories of historical fiction, reassert literature's potential to do actual good in life by way of moral example, and fueled discussions on literature's response to globalism.[5] Scholars around the world have compared Vollmann to other important contemporary figures such as Richard Powers and David Foster Wallace. In 2011, a MLA panel organized by Daniel Lukes addressed his works; a Berlin-based avant-garde magazine devoted forty pages to Vollmann in a single issue; and a critical volume appeared in France as a collection of essays on *The Rifles* edited by Françoise Palleau-Papin. Larry McCaffery and Michael Hemmingson have remained for a very long time the only US critics publishing book-length works on Vollmann. They edited *Expelled from Eden: A William T. Vollmann Reader* in 2004, and Hemmingson's critical assessment of Vollmann's oeuvre appeared in 2009. *William T. Vollmann: A Critical Companion,* a collection of scholarly essays edited by Christopher Coffman and Daniel Lukes, was published at the end of 2014 to great acclaim. In a nod to Vollmann's large fan base that has always outnumbered his critics, the companion includes brief pieces written by Vollmann enthusiasts, collaborators, and friends. Forthcoming studies on Vollmann are Michael A. T. Mellor's *William T. Vollmann: Writing America's Other Histories* and Daniel Luke's *Conversations with William T. Vollmann.*

Overview

Reading a Vollmann book is a visually stimulating and pleasing experience. The several modes he employs on the page give equal importance to the printed word and the image, whether that be the maps he draws of the locations he talks about, ink drawings of a certain flower or a scene he is describing, or photographs of the places and people he is writing about. He also deploys playful typology, increasing and decreasing font size as well as changing font type for key words or phrases that recur throughout a text. He experiments with form and textual layout, but the guiding principle is more a high-modernist preoccupation with form than an urge to experiment for experiment's sake. His books are meticulously divided into parts, chapters, and sections. In most cases, fiction and nonfiction alike, such as *Last Stories and Other Stories, Thirteen Stories and Thirteen Epitaphs* or *The Atlas* and *The Book of Dolores,* the divisions denote a structure of thematic pairing. Although the method and scope of his research methods vary from book to book, Vollmann basically reads the history and major literary works of a culture or country, focuses on their myths and religious practices, and tries to get a sense of all the forms of that society's collective identity. Conducting personal interviews and learning individual stories are crucial steps of his research. Physical experience of the landscape, climate, poverty, and danger of any given place is indispensable for him. He is confident that he can thus identify with and imagine the circumstances of the characters in his books and portray them truthfully and candidly. This holds true not only for the journalistic pieces like *Poor People* or *Imperial* but also for a historical project like the Seven Dreams series and a novel like *Whores for Gloria,* which, in Vollmann's words, "bears witness. It is a documentary in the form of a novel. All the prostitutes in the book are real people. Most of the incidents and dialogues are genuine. I have done my subject justice" (*Expelled from Eden,* 317).

The appendices are an equally important aspect of his books' structural organization because Vollmann meticulously documents almost all of his research findings. The data he collects prior to writing continues to be important once the book is written; it is offered to the reader who seeks further reading or wishes to fact-check and serves as a reminder that the material the book ruminates on or derives from has a real-world source. A typical Vollmann volume, fiction and nonfiction alike, ends with a bulky bibliography, an extensive chronology of events, a glossary, and lists of names and places. He is at once storyteller and archivist, novelist and scholar, journalist and fact-checker, linguist and librarian. While the bibliography verifies the accuracy of what we have just read, it also creates a second plane of history, or reality; we encounter the real events and figures once again after having just read the text's account of them. History is doubled in its unstoried version; fiction becomes fact. As standalone specifics or items in a list, the entries in a chronology contrast with the densely plotted account that precedes them. Readers are invited to share and pay all the attention they can to the book's serious treatment of a particular issue. Meanwhile, Vollmann's publishers almost always perceive these pages as gratuitous. When Larry McCaffery compiles a Vollmann chronology at the end of *Expelled from Eden,* he follows Vollmann's example and registers the deep time of world history. His selection of entries assembles several chronologies from Vollmann's books, and the range of history proves unsurprisingly long, for it registers the time in which Vollmann operates. McCaffery's first entry is from the primordial era, followed by the Fall, and as the stream of time moves on from prehistory to history, biographical entries from Vollmann's life and work slowly find their places. By dispersing, so to speak, Vollmann's life within the annals of human history, McCaffery pays tribute to "the world Vollmann has inhabited, literally and imaginatively" (*Expelled from Eden*, 387).

Vollmann has developed a unique approach to the representation of the past and history in his books. When he writes fiction, he does not proceed as if there is a neat division between historical fiction and fictional history or treat fact and fiction as irreconcilable. The version of the past he discovers through diligent research is rarely registered in official accounts. The central questions for him are always "How to know?," "How to represent?," "What distinguishes 'as if' from 'it was'?," and "Can we supplement history with imagination, or vice versa?" Vollmann seems to follow in the footsteps of his favorite writer, Danilo Kiš, who explains, "I distrust the arbitrariness of imagination—it is my greatest literary obsession. . . . I believe that literature must correct History: History is general, literature concrete; History is manifold, literature individual. History shows no concern for passion, crime, or numbers. What is the meaning of 'six million dead' (!) if you don't see an individual face or body—if you don't hear an individual story? . . . And how can I correct History through literature, how can I make up for History's indifference if not by using authentic documents, letters, and objects bearing the traces of real beings. . . . Documents are eyewitness reports. An eyewitness report is the best document" (*Homo Poeticus,* 205–6).

The Seven Dreams series, for instance, imagines multiple temporalities through historically faithful retellings that reject the official, monolithic versions of the past. For Vollmann, history is always history from below. History and artistry merge in Vollmann's imagination and encyclopedia-like consciousness. The factual need not destroy the imaginary–on the contrary, fact feeds fiction, especially in the case of portraying historical figures. Vollmann asserts that in the Seven Dreams series he tries to "go beyond" official histories "by making use of the novelist's tool of character," which offers "radical interpretations" of real-life persons based on "close study of sources" that recover the person as he or she "really was" (*Expelled from Eden,* 314). His novels are imaginary, but in them imagination is "appropriately filtered and disciplined" so that it remains faithful to primary historical sources (315). The single criterion for a successful historical novel for Vollmann is that it be as accurate as a history textbook—a principle he adheres to uncompromisingly throughout his oeuvre, across his novels and stories and nonfiction alike. The truly revolutionary aspect of his career may lie in his artistic representation of the factual and the way he deploys nonfiction as a tool for moral inquiry, for intellectual dialogue, and for constructive cultural and political criticism. In this way, he contributes to a powerful, albeit underrated, aspect of contemporary American letters.

Although Vollmann's ongoing, voluminous output may seem intimidating to readers, it might be surprising to learn that his books revolve around a rich but accessible set of themes that are uniquely explored afresh in each book. Vollmann's exhaustive treatment of his themes does not offer immediate and clear pronouncements. What Vollmann does instead is to meticulously examine all the various manifestations and explanations of a given issue without rushing to any conclusions, inviting the reader to think and decide along with him. Vollmann writes frequently, always comprehensively and inventively, about death, war, and violence. Conflict of any kind appeals to him immensely because if he can decipher, interpret, and put in proper context the justifications of actions, he can construct a moral chart where justifications can be held accountable, whether in the case of environmental disasters or ideological hostilities. Calling his books his "ethical laboratories" where he investigates human moral behavior, Vollmann explores how we make moral decisions and how the shifting ground between good and evil informs them.

Vollmann is committed to understanding the other and invests considerable time and effort into getting to know the foreign, the exotic, and the unknown. He prizes empathy, honesty, and trust in his encounters with people. Attending to the suffering and pain of others, finding ways to be of help are his foremost goals. Coming to understand the other is inseparable from his relentless effort to understand the self. His treatment of love and sexuality, especially in his early works, are efforts to figure basic human companionship, and being loved is always what his characters yearn for. The sexual current that runs throughout his writing is always directed toward fallen women. Vollmann's fondness for prostitutes is well known. For him, they are (semi)divine creatures (though no angels) that deserve love and sympathy: their suffering makes them sacred because it is physically, mentally, and spiritually extreme; some of them are wicked and dishonest, but most are capable of great love and forgiveness; they purify vile hearts and redeem the guilty. He does not see them as morally inferior for all their faults or shortcomings. He is not disgusted by their filth or appalled by their addictions. If anything, they are better than most people for their honesty and capacity for loving and forgiving. And it is the flickering goodness of their hearts, their yearning to love and to be loved, their unexpected tenderness that pulls at Vollmann. It seems that the good girl versus bad girl division does not exist for him, yet the appeal of errant souls is undeniable. In Vollmann's world, pursuing the sinful and the unredeemed holds the promise of redemption: his many sacred prostitutes allow him to enact a rescue fantasy that absolves of him, or fallen men, of their sins. Whores, not virgins, lead the wayward men to salvation. If, as Lacan says, we love because we want to be loved, Vollmann's fiction displays that constant yearning unabashedly. Vollmann almost seems like a twenty-first century incarnation of the amorous hero of Lady Murasaki's *The Tale of Genji,* Genji, who is a connoisseur of seduction and is always looking to love and be loved without reserve. Both Genji and Vollmann (as well as most of his male characters) love, or better, worship, multiple women at the same time. Vollmann among women is Genji reincarnate in a Hawthornian atmosphere where, as D. H. Lawrence puts it, love threatens to engulf all, the "blood love" that perfects the spirit and annuls reason (93).

Vollmann exalts nature and its spiritual dimension like a true romantic. *The Ice-Shirt, The Rifles,* and *The Dying Grass* from the Seven Dreams series as well as *The Atlas* are instances where Vollmann presents nature as structuring the workings of consciousness. The descriptions of the overwhelming beauty of Icelandic landscapes, permafrost in the North Pole, and the meadows of the Great Plains correspond to the psychological territories Vollmann charts. In *The Atlas,* especially, thoughts, reflections, and memories are absorbed in representations of nature. Ecological consciousness is another related strain in Vollmann's work; he focuses on environmental degradation, for example, in *The Rifles* and *Imperial* and on global warming and climate change in the recent *Carbon Ideologies* books, which are sure to bring him a much wider readership.

CHAPTER 2

Early Works

One way to approach Vollmann's body of writing would be to distinguish among works that focus on American subcultures and lower classes such as *Whores for Gloria* (1991), *Butterfly Stories: A Novel* (1993), and *The Royal Family* (2001), works that focus on international politics and human plight amid political strife such as *An Afghanistan Picture Show; or, How I Saved the World* (1993), *The Atlas* (1996), and *Rising Up and Rising Down* (2003), and those that rewrite history through fictionalized yet historically true accounts of real events, such as *Europe Central* (2005) and the series Seven Dreams: A Book of North American Landscapes (1990–2015).[1] None of these works can be assigned to a single genre: Vollmann heavily uses techniques from memoir, travel writing, historical research, and social reportage in fiction and nonfiction alike.

Most of Vollmann's early works demonstrate the extent to which his restless secular mind constantly wrestles with the absurdity and meaninglessness of death. The complex hold of death on Vollmann informs his equally obsessive treatments of love, sex, power, and violence. His compulsive interest in these subjects is frequently apparent in the autobiographical elements in his writing, the most prominent of which is the drowning of his six-year-old sister, Julie, in a New Hampshire pond in 1968 after the nine-year-old Vollmann had been left in charge of her while their parents were briefly away. Vollmann was reading a book by the pond, and he was immersed in his reading—a tragedy for which he blamed himself well into adulthood.

In his memoir, *An Afghanistan Picture Show; or, How I Saved the World* (written in 1982, published in 1991), Vollmann explains, "When I was growing up, my little sister drowned because I hadn't paid attention" (165). The context in which Vollmann confesses his guilt is striking: this sentence is the unspoken response to a hypothetical (and curious) question a friend of his asks while they are cruising in Alaska together: "If your child fell overboard, would you jump down and save it?" (165). Vollmann answers that it would depend on whether the child was a wanted one, hinting at undercurrents of guilt. While this cruel answer feigns indifference, a private thought revealed in the following pages makes it clear that there is more to it. Lest we doubt his willingness to help others, we read a few pages later that he went to Afghanistan because it was *invaded*. In his mind, this was a chance for him to reach out to people who were vulnerable, unprotected, in danger. His rather foolish idealism comes through in the charm that he finds in chaos and disaster; he "kept waiting for something to happen, for the black mountains to explode, for the ice to break, for thunder and lightning to come," for an opportunity to arise that would allow him to be useful but that at the same time would threaten his life (*Afghanistan*, 168). In other words, he seeks something that would make up for his failure to help Julie. Of course, it doesn't seem that he has chosen the best way to achieve that because it is a little absurd that he believes that without military training and without speaking the language he can help the mujahideen in their fight against the Soviets.[2]

Julie appears in an elusive but suggestive way in *Butterfly Stories* (1993) as well. This early, highly autobiographical, episodic novel that claims to be about the "most honest form of love called prostitution" opens in Cambodia in the late 1970s (3). The first vignette delivers in gruesome (and almost sadistic) detail the murder and torture of people trying to escape the violence of the Khmer Rouge. While Cambodians did flee to Thailand, the Cambodian minefields and mass graves that serve as background prove more personal than historical. For one, the scene is infused with spider imagery, which is a leitmotif about death in general and Julie's death in particular that Vollmann fully develops in *The Atlas* (1997). Second, *Butterfly Stories* evokes the violence of the Khmer Rouge whenever the protagonist feels guilty about failing to truly love and protect the prostitutes he falls for: searching for his missing love, Vanna, for instance, "he thought of the place where they'd suffocated babies by the hundreds, hanging them from the branches to choke inside plastic bags. He thought of the scars on Vanna's back" (251). Her existence is forever compromised in Vollmann's eyes, and only his unconditional love may help her. The idea that he can save fallen people (here, women, elsewhere, others like Afghans, the homeless, drug addicts, and so forth) to make up for his failure to save his sister resonates throughout *Butterfly Stories*.

Narrative-wise, however, the second vignette makes such a sharp transition that it denies immediate meaning or purpose to the violent images just evoked: "The butterfly boy knew nothing about this [violence in Cambodia], firstly because he was only seven years old and in another country, and secondly because it hadn't happened yet" (10). Leaving the violent scene of babies dying at the hands of Khmer Rouge and its association with Julie's lifeless body behind, the narrative switches to an account of the childhood of butterfly boy in the United States. Of course, when butterfly boy grows up, he goes to Thailand as a sex tourist and sleeps and hopelessly falls in love with women who belong to that bloody past. Apparently, he seeks more than love: he denounces protective sex when AIDS and other STDs are widespread among sex workers. If he fails to find true love, he at least tests HIV positive at the end of his trip, and we wonder whether getting lovesick and physically sick were interchangeable purposes for him or whether this is a lesson in the Vollmannian ethics of ends and means, to which Vollmann devotes a major portion of his career. The most we can say is that while he pushes the limits of loving the other (and looks for such love where it might not be possible at all), he compulsively subjects himself to brokenheartedness and makes himself vulnerable to disease, injury, and death. He seems to reverse the trope of prostitutes transmitting disease and ruining men. Such is his death drive; he can die for every woman he fails to love truly. He is ready to die any time for the sister who died needing his care, which he did not have the chance to offer: he was carried away reading his book while Julie swam to the deep end of the otherwise shallow pond.

The contrasting tone between the opening vignettes of *Butterfly Stories* is further problematized by a vague remark the protagonist makes in the second vignette about how he didn't see a dead person until he was nine. One the one hand, it foreshadows the many dead (and dying) people Vollmann / the butterfly boy will see (or pursue or dream about). On the other hand, based on circumstantial evidence, this person is Julie.[3] Although she is neither identified nor remembered in this book, the grown-up survivor's guilt-ridden, globe-traversing, self-destructive search for love circles around this primal death. If he cannot recall Julie's moment of dying—because he never saw or heard her struggle for her life—then maybe he can envision and thus remember, and even hear, other deaths. He can save others—those that otherwise seem impossible to save. The passing remark in the second vignette stresses that there is a connection between Vollmann's attraction to violent and dangerous situations (as both potential victim and savior) and the repressed memory of his childhood.

The knightly errand of saving damsels in distress, however problematically self-serving it might be, goes beyond mere fantasy for Vollmann. At one point, he comes close to executing it. In a controversial 1991 *Spin* feature, he tells how he (and Ken Miller) kidnapped a child sold into prostitution in Thailand and literally saved her. An account of this operation appears in the "No Reason to Cry" chapter of *The Atlas*. Vollmann goes to a brothel; he is put in a room with a pubescent called Ting. “I said to myself: This girl is so sad and trapped and needs my help; let me rescue her . . .” (31). Another chapter in *The Atlas,* “Under the Grass,” narrates the aftermath of this so-called heroic act. It may seem surprising that this chapter is the most explicit treatment of Julie’s death in Vollmann’s writing, but Ting’s rescue story drives home the psychological dynamics in Vollmann’s work in all their intensity, hypocrisy, and chauvinism.

Having saved Ting, he now “deserved what heroes get”: sex (*The Atlas,* 108). But he is not fussy at all: “I picked the first woman that approached me in the bar. . . . I did not care. I was simply lonely. I wanted a human being that I could touch” (108). He guesses her age sixteen, but pays for her companionship anyway. “I’ll buy you out if you want me to,” he tells her. Here he is with another underage girl, and he thinks he “was being a hero again” (108). After sleeping with the girl half-heartedly, he dreams about his mother asking him, “You mean you really don’t remember the box? and I said no, already terrified, at which my father began to tell me. He said that you [Julie] had not drowned at all. You had disappeared. After several days they finally thought to look in a large wooden box that I had left in the yard—a coffin, of course, in which you lay rotting. I woke up either screaming or thinking I was screaming. That was when I realized that everything I had done was for nothing, that no matter how many young girls I saved I could never undo or appease, that my meeting with your ghost could never be friendly because you waited to send me panic dreams whenever you could; and when I died at last, then the true punishment would begin” (108).

The timing of this moment in the brief but fragmented “Under the Grass” is crucial. The piece begins in New Hampshire the year of the fatal accident and jumps to 1993 when Vollmann rethinks the event in three movements: first as a relentless traveler at an airport in Mauritius, then as a john in the company of an underage sex worker in Thailand, and finally as a weary man wandering the catacombs in Italy. Major Vollmann themes gather around Julie’s death here: guilt; compulsive traveling; love and prostitutes; the death-wish, and the confrontation with mortality. If the victory of rescuing Ting (from men like himself) is negated in the nightmare, it is because thus far he has written about Julie using an “exclusionary conceit” (103), that is, an evasive, repressive, and repressed gesture that nonetheless obsessively circles around the event. In other words, up until now, he had not allowed himself to see the psychological underpinnings of his actions. Giving up the ghost requires Vollmann to confront his past, the content of his heart, and his self as filtered through Julie’s memory. “My blood-writing has quarried you,” he tells Julie, and *The Atlas* in its entirety seems to be an attempt to lay her to rest along with other traumas from his past.

The Atlas is an ode to memory, albeit one that proves erratic in its reconstruction of the past: with every remembrance Vollmann's mind recursively wanders among all the people he has known and loved across the world, from New York to Sarajevo, Bangkok, Nairobi, Yukon territory, Berlin, Mogadishu, Rome, and countless other cities. The book's palindromic structure and its Kawabata-inspired vignette style hold these infinitely expanding associations together. At the center is the eponymous chapter, "The Atlas." It is not part of the palindrome; it sits in the middle without a thematic twin, yet in sixty-odd pages, it manages to condense and expand on the major preoccupations of the whole book itself. In the story, set during a train ride across Canada, a land so "full of nature and loneliness," with "balsam" that promises to heal every "heart-wound or soul-wound," Vollmann's mind returns to the past (207, 203). "So many souls and countries weighing down his atlas—eternally everywhere everybody—He remembered all the women he'd loved and waited for, all the friends and hopes like fruits in the compartments of an upslanted tray" (205).

"The Atlas" delivers Vollmann's finest reflections on travel, self-questioning, remembering, forgetting, loneliness, love, sex, guilt, and especially, death. It is noteworthy that two personal losses as painful as Julie's death permeate the narrative and compel Vollmann to confront his self-destructive bent. One regards his many encounters with death while reporting on the Yugoslavian civil war and the other is the news of his first love's terminal illness. He is always the survivor, laden with guilt and encumbered by a death wish. He especially remembers his dying first love's ferocious lust for life that rolled eros and thanatos into one, her desire for "a fast, crazy, creative, destructive existence" that made her want to throw herself "out a twentieth-story window" (220). The fact that she got ill instead of him makes no sense: "How many twentieth-story windows can you throw yourself out of? he wanted to ask her. That has sometimes been my life. But unfortunately when I aim for concrete the ground always turns out to be Jell-O and goose-down and rubber. That's why you got the cancer and I didn't. Nobody can kill me. Not even I can kill me. You had already been married for years the time the bullet jammed" (220).

The bullet in question belonged to a Serbian sniper that brushed his ankle in 1992. He had traveled from Zagreb to Sarajevo many times when the fighting was fierce and barely survived two attacks en route, one in 1992 and the other in 1994. Thinking of his first love, he remembers how he rushed to every place that would bring him death and ended up among the few surviving ones. Vollmann conflates tragedies, and it seems that painful memories come in seamless clusters.

His thoughts about his first love struggling for her life soon turn into an analysis of his desire for penance. He feels so guilty that he wants to give his whole self to her. "He only wanted her to be happy if she could. If she had any notion of how he could help her, he would do whatever she asked" (221). Vollmann admits that although another former lover he remembers taught him that he is more than the proud veneer of the caring, selfless, worshipping partner, he is still so plagued by feelings of "incompleteness and emptiness" that he cannot sleep alone (237). When he confronts his "need-driven selfishness," his "desperate loneliness," he realizes that "behind his screen of consideration, sincere though it was, he operated almost ruthlessly"; his is a love with "filthy love-claws" (237).

Confronting his self-destructive and selfish bent in other contexts proves trickier. The train lulls him to sleep, and in a dream sequence that lasts about twelve pages, he struggles with more unhappy memories. There is one event that he circles around but never fully addresses here. In 1994, he tried to cross from Zagreb to Sarajevo. He hired Francis, his American-Croatian friend, a close friend from high-school, and Will, a new acquaintance, also American, to help him. They drive their car into a land mine. Francis dies immediately while Will dies slowly, in agony. Sitting in the backseat with a bulletproof vest, Vollmann witnesses everything and survives with minor injuries. In the fifth volume of *Rising Up and Rising Down,* Vollmann gives a full account of this event and details his struggle with feelings of guilt, but in "The Atlas" as well as another chapter in the book titled "Cowbells," it is described in the same understated way that Julie's accident is. Vollmann is aware that he has acted recklessly, yet he now refutes the self-destructive instincts that he had embraced a couple of pages earlier in "The Atlas": "By his own standards he was simply looking for something. He wanted to see the world, that was all. He wanted to know and love the entire atlas" (224).

By the time his train reaches Northwest Territories, Vollmann has retraversed the world, revisited all the pages of his atlas, in memory. "What, then? What had he found?" he asks (252). This is what traveling has taught him:

> No place was the end, nowhere never. The end was only in the observer's eyes. After witnessing violent deaths in the semi-elongated progress of his travels, he'd begun to gain the mystic ability to know exactly how the people he loved would die should they too be murdered. He'd be chatting with them on some innocuous subject—cumuli, the Republicans—when suddenly their hideous screams would toll in his heart; he'd see their pâté'd brains oozing greasily out of their foreheads or learn how their carotid arteries would urinate the dark liquid; he'd watch life drain from their faces with astonishing speed, the eyes going fishy and useless, the flesh becoming pale gray clay. It was always his fault. And they'd go on talking, not realizing

> that they were dead; he'd make himself smile, since it was no good warning them. Soon they'd be broken. That was destiny. And of course he remained well aware that most of these people would not die unpleasantly at all. It was all a figment of horror, some parasite overlaying their healthy countenances, defiantly exposing itself like a cartoon pervert and drinking *his* life; he, not the doomed recipients of his poisoned friendship, was the coward who died the proverbial thousand deaths. But he didn't even fear dying so much; it was more the ritual of watching them end, always in unique ways, the timbre of their screams plausibly calibrated to their well-known voices which he scarcely if ever heard raised. (257)

Francis, he explains in volume 5 of *Rising Up and Rising Down,* screamed twice before he died (443). Julie never screamed because "the fishes asked to drink your gurgling breaths" and "the sand asked to fill your mouth" (*The Atlas,* 103). Her toy, however, screamed "horrifying screams" (104). Imagined or witnessed, dying screams are what saves him eventually: "What lesson am I to learn from these screams," he wonders until he realizes that "the screams were so horrible because life was beautiful. He, the dullard, needed to be hunted by screaming throughout his life, so that the fear, agony and grief at *losing* life which they evoked would remind him to cherish it in himself and others" (259). Remembering the screams is good because remembering is living. Forgetting devours the soul like "that new virus he'd read about that converts a person into black slime in three days" (213). Traveling is living: "His mind and soul had gone so many times abroad, each time ensnaring him in new experiences from which, struggling to get free or to dig himself deeper, he'd dusted and buried his past" (214).

The pivotal role of memory and remembering in a meaningful life, which happens to be one full of suffering and despair, is the subject of another early work, a novella entitled *Whores for Gloria,* which is the tragic love story of an alcoholic Vietnam veteran that takes place in San Francisco's Tenderloin district. At about 150 pages, this is a very slim book by Vollmann's standards. It took a long time for Vollmann to find a publisher willing to publish this novella.[4] Vollmann has claimed that *Whores for Gloria* is on par with *Let Us Now Praise Famous Men* as well as *The Grapes of Wrath* in its truthful representation of human suffering and the sordid, gruesome aspects of existence. Opening with a metafictional disclaimer, the novella presents itself as the fictional counterpart of real-life tales of "despair" (*Whores for Gloria,* 1). It begins with an anecdote about a prostitute who shoots "her own watery excrement" up her veins (because she needs a substitute for heroin, as it has ceased to be effective, and she has heard the expression "shooting the shit"), which produces "magnificent abscesses" on her body. Vollmann has said in interviews that the scarred, sore, abscessed bodies of prostitutes signify remarkable resilience and endurance—they are signs of human beauty and greatness for him. He is also drawn to the agonies of unrequited love and the futile search for a lost lover, which is an ordeal many of his male characters go through and a situation he describes in a second anecdote, the "tale of the man who decided to kill himself by swallowing his athlete's foot medicine. Loving Gloria, he died in inconceivable agony." If the first anecdote is a generic red-light-district story in its evocation of a certain kind of desperation experienced by countless individuals, the other gives voice to a more specific, more private form of suffering. The trope of the lonely, lost, alcoholic Vietnam veteran acquires a new expression in Vollmann's account of the heroic struggle with inner torment and lack of human connection. In turning this man's story into fiction, he depicts our true obsession with and addiction to love without rendering it trite or sentimental. Interwoven with the imaginary reconstruction of his protagonist's life, named Jimmy, are the plain, true-to-life stories of Tenderloin sex workers, which stand like bulwarks against falsehood and meaninglessness—from them, both Vollmann and Jimmy draw a sense of reality.

Whores for Gloria has a tidy structure in contrast to Vollmann's other books, which have intricate architectures. In twenty-nine brief chapters, the novella chronicles Jimmy's desperate search for a prostitute named Gloria. Jimmy is first presented to us as an object of pity and scorn. An undercover policewoman who spots him using a payphone she knows is out of order eavesdrops on his long, forlorn monologue on the phone. We overhear, along with her, "the damned drunk" talking and pleading through tears, "lean[ing] forward inside the phone booth as if that would somehow diminish the distance between him and the person he was talking to" (5). She considers him a nuisance, but Jimmy's affectionate manner and immersion in his imaginary world affects her; she stops looking for signs of criminal activity on the street and begins daydreaming about her upcoming vacation to Hawaii with her husband, swimming in the ocean like a mermaid in the corals and conversing with schools of fish. At the same time, she registers Jimmy's emotional turmoil: "His voice was very low and gentle and even. His voice was patient and tender" (5–6). He showers his imaginary listener with affection. After hanging up "very carefully and gently," the man makes another call and books a plane ticket for Gloria "because she can't take care of herself she needs help in everything she does" (7). Desperate to be needed by some other soul, desperate to love, this man is not much different than the policewoman: the sane and the insane both crave companionship, make optimistic plans for the future, and surrender often to the dream worlds of wild flight and happiness with a loved one.

In subsequent chapters we see Jimmy drinking and asking everyone about Gloria's whereabouts. After he became an alcoholic, he forgot all about the war, and now "he wanted to be drunk enough to scientifically establish the existence of the whores that he could see all around him" (10). Every time Jimmy fails to locate Gloria, he attempts to "remember" her (21). In other words, decides to live his relationship with her in the imaginary realm. First, he needs memories. He begins to pay for company in the literal sense, hiring prostitutes to hear them recount pleasant memories from their childhood. "Tell me some happy stories about when you were a girl" Jimmy asks a girl named Melissa, who complies, although her memories turn out to be very ordinary accounts of her first train ride, her first movie theater visit, and her first puppy (25). Jimmy reveres these banalities, and before he goes to sleep that night, he recounts every memory Melissa has relayed to him and imagines having experienced the occasions she described with Gloria when they were both children. He moves beyond the romantic and erotic in extending his relationship with Gloria to his childhood, creating a meaningful past and life for himself with the help of this absent woman. "God help me to give up food," he prays, "so that I can spend more of my SSI checks on whores and find what I need to find and God let Gloria grow right with me because I sure don't want to die alone" (19).

His insistence on happy childhood stories is significant because he understands that prostitutes are unhappy, just like he is; his thinking seems to be that if only they can tell him their happy memories and prove that they had been happy, innocent, and content once, he can be happy, too. Jimmy may think that both he and the prostitutes have had difficult lives but that now that is over and they can be happy again. Or perhaps this is Jimmy challenging life, offering proof of a relentless optimism that happiness is still possible. He believes he might learn "secret good things about the whores that make memories worthy of Gloria" (104). Holding on to Gloria requires that he hold on to the possibility of hope and happiness. As the narrator remarks, "We must all build our worlds around us, bravely or dreamily, as long as we can shelter ourselves from the rain, walling ourselves in gorgeously" (45). Jimmy's world is built out of dreams, since he has nothing else.

After a while, Jimmy tires of trying to fabricate a past with Gloria out of disconnected pieces and decides to reserve the happy memories to himself. He thinks, "if he heard enough happy stories and put them in his *own* memory-bank then maybe he wouldn't need Gloria anymore" (103). However, memories of just himself prove to be worthless for his purposes, even if they are happy ones. "The problem he said to himself is how can I put one foot ahead of the other day after day for the rest of my life?" (107). He asks a prostitute to tell him "sad stories. I need 'em sad so I can make 'em happy" (132). The novel closes with Jimmy drifting from woman to woman, his quest for Gloria the subject of ridicule. Rumors of his death eventually spread, and everyone believes that Gloria found and killed him. *Whores for Gloria* can be seen as an account of the human effort to transcend a lonely, loveless, and meaningless life. There is a heartbreaking beauty in Jimmy's obsession with human connection, mutual care and love, belief in and devotion to the idea that there is meaning in life. At the end of the novella, Vollmann documents the real-life foundations of what we have just read. He provides snippets of interviews with real street prostitutes that address various aspects of the profession. During Jimmy's pursuit to find the missing, imaginary woman, many flesh-and-blood women step forward and offer the forlorn lover their compassion and understanding. Through the stories they tell Jimmy, they themselves emerge as creatures who yearn as much as he does and who have experienced as much heartbreak as him. Vollmann challenges us to seek insight into the heart and mind of the other, with whom we may or may not sympathize, to find a way to acknowledge that they are complex human beings.

Whores for Gloria stands in Vollmann's oeuvre as an early but signature treatment of sex workers and subcultures. He seems especially interested in understanding how these people search constantly for love and fail to find it. Vollmann explains in a 1989 biographical statement that his interest in "underdogs and doomed causes" turned into an all-encompassing interest in many forms of subcultures, sustained by his realization that "love is what they all want. But they do not know how to get it, and so they become twisted. Must life be like this for so many people? Does it come about from the way people are or the way people live? Was it always this way?" (*Expelled from Eden,* 5). Hoping to gain insight into their doomed quests for human connection, Vollmann spends extensive amounts of time with them. For instance, in an essay from 1993, "Honesty," Vollmann describes his first impressions of San Francisco's street walkers. He was "saddened and appalled: the dirt, the disease, the hard carapace over the fearful soul, the hatred, the danger, the addiction, the premature death" (64). His initial shock at and disgust with these women's unclean, damaged bodies turns into a fascination with their resilience—skin mutilated with burns and various scars, body deformed with hunger and bloating testify to their ability to endure horrible physical pain. "When I see a woman's body covered," Vollmann notes, "with abscesses, needle tracks, motorcycle scars, bruises and bullet wounds, I experience awe at the endurance of this person in the teeth of the forces of which her flesh bears witness. When I see a younger girl just beginning the trade, reeking so richly of sex, I glimpse her as an icon of what makes and renews us, a literal fertility goddess, the perpetuation of life" (65–66). But, perhaps more important, Vollmann exalts these women's peace with their disfigured, abject bodies. Their ease becomes his ease; they alleviate his self-consciousness about his skin scarred with acne. A prostitute's body becomes an emblem of honesty for Vollmann because it proves that "the person stands beyond and above the body" (66). The prostitutes he encounters and befriends teach him "how to be free." It is to these women and others that Vollmann turns again and again in order to draw from their stories confidence and strength, like *Whores for Gloria's* Jimmy.

CHAPTER 3

Kissing the Mask, The Book of Dolores

In "The Shame of It All: Some Thoughts on Prostitution in America" (1999), Vollmann confesses that he cannot "truly claim to understand" sex workers (*Expelled from Eden,* 168). He goes on to ask: "What is she? What is she? 'But what is a woman *emotionally* and *spiritually*?'—Who's wise enough to answer that?" (169). Anyone who has heard about Vollmann has probably also heard that he writes a lot about sex workers and red-light zones across the globe—and that he writes from experience. To some, he is a decadent par excellance. To others, he is a humanist sui generis. Given that he writes so much about women and his encounters with them, a fair question is what is a woman to Vollmann? The answer is complex, but two mature works of nonfiction may be a good place to start.

Any Vollmann book is as much storytelling as it is research. When and if he cannot dig into the archive, he hits the street—whether that be the North Magnetic Pole, the Tenderloin, Cambodia, or brothels in Thailand and everywhere else. There have, however, been times when both archival and field research failed him. While working on *How You Are,* an unpublished novel about a male-to-female Mexican sex worker, nothing seemed to help him get into the head (and heart) of his transgender heroine. He was unable to put himself into the shoes of a woman or those of a man becoming a woman—sex worker or not. In Vollmann's moral universe, this is a crime against empathy.

Vollmann completed the manuscript of *How You Are* about a decade ago, but, interestingly, no publication date has yet been specified. But his research for the novel generated two works of nonfiction, *Kissing the Mask* (2010) and *The Book of Dolores* (2013). In these books, Vollmann asks "What is a woman?" and his efforts to answer this question show that he is an empath trying to know the radical other, the woman. Beyond this shared inquiry, *Kissing the Mask* and *The Book of Dolores* have little in common. While the first explores performances of femininity, focusing on men impersonating women in art and in daily life, and can best be classified as a hybrid work of sociology and anthropology, the latter attempts at a performance of femininity itself and belongs, however problematically, to the genre of self-portraits. Collectively taken, these books show that Vollmann treats gender as an unstable entity, and he insinuates that his original question is moot.[1] In *Kissing the Mask,* he even talks about "the possible genderlessness of the soul, whose most appropriate reification might be that ancient Hungarian figurine whose shape was of an erection with testicles but whose glans was a woman's face and whose long neck bore hard-nippled little breasts almost halfway down; the scrotum was a woman's buttocks" (244).

The mask in the title of *Kissing the Mask* refers to one of the female masks worn by actors in the all-male Japanese Noh theater. The full title of the book is thirty-four words long: *Kissing the Mask. Beauty, Understatement and Femininity in Japanese Noh Theater—With Some Thoughts on Muses (Especially Helga Testorf), Transgender Women, Kabuki Goddesses, Porn Queens, Poets, Housewives, Makeup Artists, Geishas, Valkyries and Venus Figurines.* The title signals how wide a net Vollmann casts in his pursuit of ancient and contemporary aspects of femininity. Vollmann's interest in Japanese culture is well known, and his courage in attempting to learn its intricacies is admirable, for it is a highly specialized topic of inquiry by all accounts.[2] Like in *The Atlas* or *Rising Up and Rising Down,* Vollmann travels around the globe, now in search of beauty's gender-bending manifestations: transvestites in Los Angeles, Japanese crossdressers, and feminine norms and expressions of feminine beauty in Old Norse, Hellenistic, Indian, and Western European cultures.

Vollmann's focus on Noh drama may seem a bizarre choice for a study of femininity given that women are barred from acting in Noh. It is this fact, however, that attracts Vollmann: Noh relies on enactments of feminine elegance, or "precisely modulated" grace, by mostly elderly male actors whose manly necks and feet remain visible (2). However, the actors do not turn into ordinary women on stage when they wear masks, kimonos, and wigs: each mask designates a distinctive woman of a certain age and a specific sexual and marital status and comes with a strict set of gestures and emotions that the actor must perform to properly impersonate the various types of women. Insofar as Noh is a reservoir of centuries-long definitions of multiple representations of femininity, it presents an inexhaustible source of information for Vollmann's examination of the performative aspects of feminine gender. In the process, Vollmann interviews Noh actors, a female Noh mask maker, geishas, and heterosexual women and meditates on muses inspiring artists in order to compose a history of what is called feminine beauty. His personal muse seems to be the mask of a prepubescent girl, a *ko-omote,* tantalizing him with a kiss.

Kissing the Mask is a classic Vollmann book in its obsessive treatment of an arcane topic, authorial self-insertion, a substantial set of illustrations, and generous appendices (notes, chronology, bibliography, glossary sections). It also establishes itself as a rare and edifying sourcebook on Noh theater, supplying an introduction to its centuries-long history and rules, nice summaries of various plays, and catalogues of Noh masks. Just as the Seven Dreams novels could well serve any history buff, so too would *Kissing the Mask* be a useful resource for anyone interested in this ancient Japanese art of staged femininity. The allure of Noh for Vollmann is that the texts and the choreographies of the plays have not been altered since conception many centuries ago: "The role is eternal. The mask is, practically speaking, nearly eternal: longer than a single human life" (33). We are faced with unchanging representations of femininity, then, and Vollmann is after its secrets, its timeless standards, if there is such a thing.

The highlight of *Kissing the Mask* may be the chapter entitled "They Just Want to Look in the Mirror: Yukiko Makes Me Over." After watching Noh actors and geishas get made up and dressed for the enactment of perfect femininity, Vollmann now takes his turn. He visits the salon of Yukiko, an underground beautician in Tokyo. Cross-dressers who want to keep their secrets safe visit Yukiko in the evening hours for a short drag session before they return to their duties as fathers and husbands: Yukiko applies makeup and provides wigs, and, most importantly, gives the men a mirror with which they gaze at their own crafted femininities. When it's Vollmann's turn to sit, she carefully conceals Vollmann's coarse skin with layers upon layers of cosmetics, draws arched eyebrows, applies lipstick, and puts on his head a wig. Next, Vollmann gazes at himself in the mirror and takes photographs of himself: "It seems that a woman is looking back at me—not a beautiful woman, perhaps, but still, here is someone who came into the world just now and will exist more briefly than I, a woman who has feelings (my feelings); she wants to look her best" (225). While he recognizes the woman in the mirror as a person equipped with the props to offer a spot-on performance of femininity, he does not know her: "I am other," Vollmann concludes about his cross-dressing episode.

The Book of Dolores opens with a photograph of Vollmann's makeover from this day in Tokyo. She is introduced as Dolores, a "young woman," "an aspect of myself" (12, 15). Page after page Vollmann offers us photographs and watercolor and ink drawings of Dolores, or himself in drag. He looks at her, contemplates her image, and compares her appearance with how she feels she looks. Dolores remains in the third person throughout this book of self-portraits. Vollmann never grants agency to this woman he literally morphs into, although he envisions himself as Dolores.

Why does Vollmann chronicle his experiments with cross-dressing? For one thing, the woman he writes about in *How You Are,* Dolores, is also him—to the extent that he has managed to imagine being her. For another, it is these transformations that fuel *How You Are:* the experiences of one Dolores shaped and informed the other's. Vollmann wants to arrive at an understanding of a transgender sex worker's daily life—all the hardships she suffers in public and on the street at night as well as the joys of female bonding—and the best way he can do that is by literally embodying Dolores for a while. About one third of the book is reserved for documenting instances where Vollmann as Dolores inspired certain passages and episodes in the writing of *How You Are.* They are strikingly visual in nature: how Vollmann perceives Dolores seems to have helped the imaginative process.

Perhaps one reason why *How You Are* remains unpublished is the reaction among Vollmann's circle of acquaintances to his cross-dressing. While he blissfully walked the fluid boundaries of gender, some people around him thought that he was degrading himself. It may seem curious that people who have tolerated Vollmann's friendships with homeless people, skinheads, drug addicts, and sex workers found his cross-dressing humiliating. The reaction of his friends to his cross-dressing is similar to the hostility trans people in general face, but Vollmann does not pursue the implications any further.

The Book of Dolores carries the irresolute conclusions of *Kissing the Mask* forward by treating the performative aspects of gender, at least the female gender. Vollmann believes that he, or anyone for that matter, can put on a female self in the way an elderly Noh actor does by wearing a mask and behaving in a conventionally feminine way. In almost every photograph, Dolores sports different wigs, earrings, collars, and necklaces and projects an attitude she thinks matches the look; the party girl, housewife, and geologist sequence early in the book proves the success of Dolores not as a woman but as an individual hyperaware of the multitude of gender roles available to her when she assumes a feminine aspect, however subjectively that may be defined.

It is safe to say that Vollmann has pushed the limits of the outrageous and the sensational for many people, but in the list of his outlandish acts, cross-dressing may not rank very high. For one, it seems to be research, and in that sense it is no different from his throwing himself into dangerous circumstances to carry out magazine assignments and war correspondence. For another, it puts theory into practice and allows him to test the performative boundaries of gender: he performs in the way he believes women perform but fails to discover the essence of femininity. Without a doubt, a reader unfamiliar with

Vollmann may be put off by this straight, married man with a teenage daughter flaunting his cross-dressing. "I am a heterosexual male with a hypertrophy of the empathetic organs," Vollmann explains. "Not only am I physically and emotionally attracted to women, I also wonder what being a woman would be like" (*The Book of Dolores,* 15). Why should cross-dressing not be another form of participative research if Vollmann thinks it is the only way to get to know his fictional Dolores? And what author would not champion the importance of empathy to his or her work? Indeed, the overall project of *The Book of Dolores* encapsulates how Vollmann constructs his own identity: "Because I am myself a fantasist in my capacity both as fiction writer and as an empath, someone who considers it the duty of a world citizen to step into the other person's shoes, I discreetly defy preordained places and identities" (52). In this sense, *The Book of Dolores* is a product as well as a chronicle of Vollmann's education in *How You Are,* where, he explains, "I tried to imagine myself, or a character based in part upon myself, as a woman. . . . I thought to embody some of my new conclusions and meditations about gender in the form of a woman whose circumstances require her to define herself in relation to maleness" (52).[3]

However, for a writer who invests so much time and effort into research prior to writing for the sake of accuracy, he uncharacteristically turns his blind eye to the massive theoretical corpus on gender and cross-dressing. He absolves Dolores and himself of acquiring a systematic understanding of gender and sexuality. Vollmann refuses to theorize on gender while bending it and treats his own subjective experience as the only truth when it comes to Dolores. In other words, he discovers the performative aspect of femininity anew through his subjective experiment. What offenses and hostilities a rather unattractive transgender street woman endures on a daily basis seem more important to him than any theoretical writing about gender and sexuality would say about her.

The central feature of the book is its lavishly illustrated pages, but there is also a considerable amount of text in it. Vollmann never lets Dolores alone: his gaze is on her all the time, and he comments on almost every single image reproduced, enveloping her. We do see Dolores for ourselves through her numerous photographs and imprints, but she is never a relatable subject, a character, for us. She is a construct of and for Vollmann, and it is he who tells us about her emotions. We are either witnessing Vollmann's growing empathy with Dolores or the creation of an imaginary character. In addition, the fact that it is his own male gaze that examines, judges, describes, creates, and chases femininity turns his exploration into an unintentional deconstructive gesture at times: Dolores escapes Vollmann's gaze even when he is equipped with the camera lens. The flash obscures her, or because she takes off Vollmann's glasses, he cannot see her in the mirror (which of course means she cannot see herself either, but she doesn't seem to have any problems with that). That is to say, if not for his seeing her, Vollmann could not even know her.

The Book of Dolores seems to treat the text as supplementary to the images. Vollmann describes every image in lush pictorial detail; for every photograph, block print, and watercolor drawing there is a story to tell about the production technique, the setting of the image, and the episodes from *How You Are* that it inspired. This book is not a mere photo book, because Vollmann brings Dolores to life by encountering her physically in the dark room and on paper.[4] That is why one of the most haunting things about the book is the gulf between how Dolores feels and how she actually looks in the photographs. She never looks as pretty as she feels. For all her dangling earrings, powder, paint, and sexy clothes, she never is the woman she feels herself to be in Vollmann's bespectacled eyes, which have encountered multifarious manifestations of feminine beauty. But if we were to ask who Dolores is, Vollmann would shut us down by saying that Dolores is who he is and is not. Vollmann appears trapped in a man's body, letting Dolores free only when he hits the shutter or paints her. He has to see Dolores with his *male* eyes to know her. Does that mean he has failed to empathize with her, with women, or with the heroine of *How You Are*? Maybe he is just treating Dolores like one of the people who pose for him; perhaps he thinks that like the photograph of the Alabama tenants who posed for Walker Evans in *Let Us Now Praise Famous Men,* the image of her will tell more about who she is than anything written about her could. Ultimately, even in his female persona, the essence of femininity evades Vollmann.

After all, he is trying to find a way to represent a transgender woman and personally experience "her," and he does not pretend to understand the biological woman. He took a similar approach in order to write about John Franklin and his failed expedition in *The Rifles,* for instance. What would it feel like to be an unattractive Mexican transgender sex worker cruising the night, Sir John Franklin looking for the Northwest Passage, or an illegal immigrant diving into a toxic river to cross the border? As he puts it in *Kissing the Mask,* "Can't a man praise the woman he loves? Can't he describe her? Without presuming to be her, or to know her as she knows herself, can't he claim acquaintanceship with her moods and ways?" (2). Vollmann does not consider himself an authority on the subject he explores in *Kissing the Mask* either: "Deaf, dumb and illiterate in Japanese, innocent of formal study in any discipline of art, a graceless dancer afflicted with bad eyesight, I may not be the perfect author for any essay on Noh drama" (1). Despite remarks like this, however, Vollmann did undertake exhaustive research for both *Kissing the Mask* and *The Book of Dolores* as he did with his other books, namely, by immersing himself in raw experience: the process of learning and exploring while writing is what provides understanding, however limited it may be. Research does not have to be performed beforehand. It can generate itself in the process of writing.

Perhaps it is the man visible behind Dolores and the Noh character in a mask that renders the performance of femininity so mystifying for Vollmann: gender is most stable when its boundaries are blurred. The masculine necks and feet of elderly Noh actors do not taint the pure femininity of the mask; likewise the beauty of Dolores is manifested in her effortless transformation of the male biological body into the female gender. If the mask, the kimono, the fan, and the rigidly held and moved body bestow perfect femininity on a Noh actor, so do wigs, breast forms, eyeshadow, and dresses on Dolores—the man visible behind the performance is simply beyond the reality of the performance. And that is enough for Vollmann to qualify as femininity.

CHAPTER 4

Poor People, Imperial

In *Journey into the End of the Night,* Céline observes that "poor people never, or hardly ever, ask for an explanation of all they have to put up with" (qtd. in *Poor People,* xiv). Vollmann entertains the possibility that if someone were to ask them directly about their circumstances, they might be induced to ponder them. "Why are you poor?" he asks impoverished people in Afghanistan, Pakistan, Yemen, Thailand, China, Japan, Colombia, Bosnia, Serbia, the Republic of Congo, Kenya, Russia, Kazakhstan, Mexico, and the United States, among other countries.[1] *Poor People* compiles the answers, most of which turn out to be narrow in their analytical range and seem shockingly repetitive across cultures. The first chapter, entitled "Self-Definitions," uses the resignation of the poor to think about the reasons of their poverty. Most think they are poor because there are no jobs or because the rich steal from them. Others believe it is destiny: bad karma, divine retribution, God's will. When people are disadvantaged, they prefer to normalize their plight rather than subject it to moral and intellectual analysis. But "people who are poor but not in imminent danger of perishing have more of a chance of catching their breath and actually conceptualizing their poverty," Vollmann argues (xv).[2] His goal, then, is to understand how poverty impoverishes the soul and the mind.

Vollmann is equally disheartened by the amount of uncritical thinking, or "stock thinking" as he puts it, that shapes prevalent approaches to and definitions of poverty. He quotes I. A. Richards' account of mediocre poetry to make his point about stock thinking. With a stock poem, "every item and every strand of meaning, every cadence and every least movement of the form is fatally and irrevocably familiar to anyone with any acquaintance with English poetry . . . the mental movements out of which they are composed have long been parts of our intellectual and emotional repertory, and . . . these movements are few and simple and arranged in an obvious order" (qtd. in *Poor People,* 238).

Without pretending to define poverty, Vollmann attempts to revise our understanding of it. To that end, he offers a tentative, more nuanced set of symptoms of poverty in light of what he has seen around the world. Vollmann disputes the UN's definition of poverty in terms of a short life expectancy, illiteracy, exclusion, and a lack of material resources and instead suggests eight ways in which poverty manifests itself: invisibility, deformity, unwantedness, dependence, accident proneness, pain, numbness, and estrangement (*Poor People,* 101). Each of these symptoms is suggested to Vollmann by his observation of the common experiences of the poor around the world: "Any primary source is precious, being near to reality itself" (xv). Each emerges out of the story of a poor person, some more memorable and haunting than others in their embodiment of these signs: Sunee, a middle-aged Thai cleaning woman who drinks herself to oblivion every night; Wan, a young Thai beggar with an empty gaze who claims she is rich; the eighty-one-year-old Russian beggar Oksana supporting her son who suffers from various radiation-caused maladies he acquired after working as a cleaner in Chernobyl, as well as his son's wife and two young daughters who are equally sick.

One of the strengths of *Poor People* is Vollmann's trademark proximity to its subject matter. Not only do his encounters with poor people around the world inform his writing, but his own experiences with poverty, a staple of his daily life, do as well. Vollmann lives much closer to the homeless and the poor than many well-off people (and closer than many well-off people would ever consider living themselves). "I am a petty-bourgeois property owner," Sacramento resident Vollmann explains. "My building is an old restaurant on a corner parking lot just under the railroad bridge from the homeless shelter. People sleep in my parking lot. Some of them stay for months; others I see only once" (263). He is aware that he is financially secure, if not wealthy, and safe from the fear and hopelessness poverty brings, but he is not immune to its uglier aspects. He greets the residents of his parking lot every time he sees them and shakes their hands whether they reek of excrement or not, and so does his daughter with his encouragement when she visits. He also regularly gives them money for food and drinks. Yet allowing the homeless to camp on his property also means he has to wash urine off the walls of his building, hang steel mesh over his door, and keep windows shut and blinds drawn all the time. All these precautions are results of bad experiences. He takes pains to keep homeless people out of his studio without denying them the shelter of his private property. He is realistic about the limits of his sympathy but refuses to treat the poor as if they were invisible, inferior.

Although Vollmann never claims that he has any systemic solution to poverty, he does believe in helping people on a case-by-case basis, even though helping poor people turns out to be very difficult, impractical, and possibly useless. For instance, if he gives Sunee money to pay for the education of her daughter, Sunee will quickly spend all of it on cheap whiskey. If the underlying question throughout is whether there is an effectual way to help the poor, Vollmann's conclusion is an honest, sad negative, based on his experiences in his home and around the world.

He embraces a moral principle of equality to counter such hopelessness in his interactions with the poor, detailed in the last part of the book, "Placeholders." The first section, "I Know I am Rich," is Vollmann's vividly rendered log of experiences with people camping in his parking lot. He confronts his general attitude toward the poor, admits his biases and fears, and makes a self-assessment of his egalitarianism as a rich man. Vollmann sees that he and the poor are equals in moral and emotional terms, and so he resists reducing them to mere victims of inequality. He holds them as accountable as he would any other person: "Because I wish to respect poor people's perceptions and experiences, I refuse to say that I know their good better than they; accordingly, I further refuse to condescend to them with the pity that either pretends they have no choices at all, or else, worse yet, gilds their every choice with my benevolent approval. Once again I submit the obvious: Poor people are no more and no less human than I; accordingly, they deserve to be judged and understood precisely as do I myself" (170).

Unlike James Agee, who, Vollmann claims, put his subjects on a pedestal, Vollmann does not idealize the poor. Their imperfection seems barely tolerable at times, as he deals with pools of urine at his door and acts of vandalism to his property. Vollmann feels disrespected and exploited, but he nevertheless is doubtful of his entitlement to such sentiments: "I was kind to them in ways that cost me little. Then I went across the parking lot and shut my steel door on them. Was that right?" (271). When they pound on his door with what he guesses are suspect motives, the writer who went to Afghanistan to fight with the rebels and save the world now wonders, "Was it my task to save everybody on earth?" (283).

The set of questions he asks enables him to understand the consciousness of the subjects whose cryptic words he faithfully reports. His primary goal has always been to find ways to help others by writing about things no one else has dared to write about. Whether there's a strain of self-importance in that endeavor is left to the reader to judge. Nevertheless, he is unfailing in his efforts to present as many subjectivities as possible, not just his own reflections about his encounters, in order to arrive at truths. Whether he fears or loves the poor, eventually it is their own experiences that speak in the narrative. When these broken-down dialogues are printed, a rift opens in the textual space as far as human communication goes: Vollmann's best efforts at understanding poverty are countered by the poor's willful refusal to give it rational meaning: poverty defies the realm of the mind for the poor.

Vollmann concedes that the leisure to contemplate, read, and write is a rich person's indulgence. Still, the fact that he reaches out to them, inquires about their lives in a sincere and respectful manner, and befriends them during the short time they spend together qualifies as a form of human connection for Vollmann. In addition, he frequently employs translators and reports their interpretations of poor people's descriptions of poverty as well. Translators bridge more than gaps in communication: they exemplify that particular culture's outlook on poverty when they scold or pity the interviewees, helping Vollmann measure the poverty of interviewees against that culture's norms of poverty, or what Vollmann dubs "normality" in the brief dictionary of terms that he supplies: "the local context from which relative poverty, individual well being and other such abstractions ought to be considered" (xxi).

What really methodologically drives the book are the brief conversations Vollmann enters into with thinkers and writers who have written on poverty, such as Aristotle, Montaigne, Adam Smith, and most importantly, James Agee. Any assessment of *Poor People* has to take into account *Poor People*'s literary kinship with James Agee and Walker Evans's classic study of Depression-era tenant farmers *Let Us Now Praise Famous Men* (1941). The moral and literary program of *Poor People* and the artistic consciousness and conscience of Vollmann, are defined, most powerfully in the introduction, in relation to the achievements and shortcomings of *Let Us Now Praise Famous Men.*

To begin, we should note that some books, including *Let Us Now Praise Famous Men,* have inspired Vollmann so much that he has attempted to match or even surpass their achievements. For instance, he posits that the only work close in scope and importance to *Rising Up and Rising Down* is Edward Gibbon's majestic *The History of the Decline and Fall of the Roman Empire.* He calls *Imperial* his *Moby-Dick.*[3] Another model is John Steinbeck's novel *The Grapes of Wrath.* Although *Let Us Now Praise Famous Men* did not receive attention until the 1960s when civil rights advocates discovered it, both it and *The Grapes of Wrath* are now recognized as groundbreaking documentary works of the 1930s, also known as the "documentary decade" (Wolff, 29).[4]

Vollmann's vision of literature as social history and his commitment to being a first-hand witness of his subject matter is informed by the commitment to the representation of the unadorned facts of the lives of the laborers and migrants in the West and the sharecroppers during the devastating 1930s that Steinbeck and Agee respectively model. It is possible that Steinbeck's approach to writing *The Grapes of Wrath* is an influence on Vollmann's writing methods as well: "I've done my damndest to rip a reader's nerves, I don't want him satisfied. . . . I tried to write this book the way lives are being lived not the way books are written. . . . Throughout I've tried to make the reader *participate* in the actuality, what he takes from it will be scaled entirely on his own depth or hollowness" (178). Vollmann's experiences during research dictate the structure of his books. In other words, experience dictates form. Agee tries to give the reader a sense of the extreme discomfort he experienced interacting with tenant families by conveying as much of the shocking aspects of their lives as possible. For Agee as for Vollmann, it is these shocking elements that are invisible, and by making them visible, they shake us out of our complacency. In Agee's case, of course, the gap between himself and the people he wrote about caused him immense pain and guilt. Vollmann may be much more accustomed to life on the fringes, and he does not tend to convey the same level of anguish in relaying the shocking aspects of the life of the poor.

Where Steinbeck and Agee differed eventually mattered more to Vollmann, as we see in his introduction to *Poor People,* where he seems to come to terms with his two literary patriarchs. While Steinbeck's approach epitomizes an empathy-driven, ethical form of research that turns itself confidently into fiction, Agee's demonstrates the difficulties with and fallacies of such easy fictioneering. This is a conflict Vollmann shares, but he aligns more with Steinbeck and treats Agee's failures as problems he himself managed to overcome after painful self-questioning.

While Vollmann considers his short novel *Whores for Gloria* to be in the same league as *The Grapes of Wrath* and *Let Us Now Praise Famous Men,* he thinks of his nonfiction *Poor People* as a project built on the strengths and weaknesses of both. If *Whores for Gloria* is an early work that displays Vollmann's lifelong commitment to writing fiction informed and dictated by the factual, *Poor People* is a mature work in which Vollmann seems to have perfected his documentary narrative and storytelling techniques. However, *Poor People*'s success owes considerably to its anxieties. Vollmann is in a rush to distance himself from Agee's sense of guilt—Agee, in Vollmann's view, was an educated white man who remained an elitist despite his egalitarian spirit. He was not poor, and for all his efforts he could not represent the poor; he was not capable of true affection towards the poor: his sentiment was rather a mere "childlike love," the kind that "impels a child to embrace a stranger's legs" (*Poor People,* xii). Vollmann bluntly calls *Let Us Now Praise Famous Men* "an elitist expression of egalitarian longings" (xii). Agee and Evans fail because they remain "two rich men observing the lives of the poor" (xii). Steinbeck, in contrast, comes from an underprivileged background and possesses an empathy that he cultivates during his encounters with the poor. Vollmann himself solves the problem of his distance from poor people by acknowledging that although he is not poor, he treats poor people as "fellow human beings" above all else (xiv). He is not oblivious to class distinctions but tries to find a way to connect with these people in which class does not figure.

Vollmann's rather harsh reaction to and impatience with Agee is a curious case, since *Let Us Now Praise Famous Men* is a self-acknowledged influence on his documentary nonfiction. Is *Poor People*, then, wildly different from its precursor? Many similarities suggest themselves in method and content. For one, Agee's emphasis on earning the love and trust of people whose lives he writes about seems to have influenced Vollmann's approach in seeking intimacy with his subjects. They are both very kind and friendly to people they interview; both want to become a part of their lives—however temporarily—rather than remain detached observers.[5] Theirs is participative journalism that pushes the professional boundaries of reportage toward a personal connection beyond class, race, gender. Travelogue and journalism become memoir or autobiography as the authors' highly individual response to what they have seen and heard gets filtered subjectively: both authors meditate on the extent to which they can truly know and accurately write about the people and situations they encounter. The dilemmas that arise for Vollmann by drawing fictional characters based on real-life people is well known. Agee's work is not preparatory research for a novel, but he seems deeply committed to the idea of truthful representation of the people he meets. Agee writes of a tenant: "Somehow a much more important, and dignified, and true fact about him than I could conceivably invent, though I were an illimitably better artist than I am, is the fact that he is exactly, down to the last inch and instant, who, what, where, when and why he is. . . . The one deeply exciting thing to me about Gudger is that he is actual, he is living, at this instant. He is not some artist's or journalist's or propagandist's invention: he is a human being: and to what degree I am able it is my business to reproduce him as the human being he is; not just to amalgamate him into some invented, literary imitation of a human being" (233, 240).

They differ, however, on their self-perception as observers and reporters. Agee is uncomfortable with his position as an alien intruding on the tenants' lives and considers himself a "spy" exploiting already disadvantaged people. He despairs over earning the trust of his interviewees—a trust he thinks he does not deserve to receive. In contrast, Vollmann rarely has such qualms and envisions a smoother bonding process in his encounters. He is obviously proud of the hard-won trust he has earned among poor people. Being honest is the golden rule of journalism for Vollmann. Both Agee and Vollmann want to call their subjects friends—they value establishing intimate connections with those who are radically other. The difference is, Agee feels too much sadness for the poor and too much shame over his privilege; Vollmann says he wishes to help other people whenever he can, and he tries to treat class difference matter of factly without assuming superiority.

Nonetheless, Vollmann has been criticized for exploiting his interviewees because he pays them to answer his questions. In *Poor People,* after he says that he "was paying for these interviews," he makes an offensive aside in a footnote: "That's right! I was paying for them; I was rich! Didn't that give my invasiveness carte blanche? In *Let Us Now Praise Famous Men,* Evans and Agee inspected every inch of their subjects' houses while the latter were away at church. Only you, reader, can decide whether such knowledge as you gain from reading that long passage of the book justifies its means" (16).

Vollmann justifies compensating his subjects for their time answering his questions on the grounds that he is helping them out by paying them, and they are helping him in return. Despite copious attention to the material circumstances of their lives, Vollmann denies that he objectifies their possessions or dwellings, arguing that what they own and where they live are useless details when it comes to understanding the hearts and minds of these people. Furthermore, he considers it a breach of trust to subject their lives to such disrespectful scrutiny: whatever is known about them should be given knowingly and willingly to the intruder. "All I can say is that I'm moved by other people's misfortunes, and I feel obliged to record them unflinchingly. If anyone thinks I exploited these people, I hope they think about how I did it, and how they could do better by them" (16). Paying for interviews establishes an economy of equals between a pursuer of knowledge and the possessor of it. "I was paying for these interviews," Vollmann continues, "because I wanted to learn something which might benefit others." In 2014 he told an interviewer that he is never sure if for all his efforts he has actually managed to help people. "That's the crazy, haunting thing" in Vollmann's life: the return of the irrepressible feeling that he has failed (307). If Agee's guilt over the misfortunes of the other exhausts his potential to truly connect, it is guilt as well as the compulsion to help the errant and the shamefaced that enables and motivates Vollmann.

To further elaborate, an important aspect of Vollmann's radical openness to the other is the extreme emotional and physical proximity he maintains with his subjects during his research and interviews. While this is responsible for the sensational element in his writing, it also illuminates his problematic relationship with women. Haunted by his guilt over Julie's death, Vollmann seeks the forgiving affection of every woman he encounters. All are dear to him. And he wants to be loved by them all. So it is forgiveness, the saintly love of a whore as well as the virgin, that he seeks as much as pleasure. Agee has similar passion for forgiveness, albeit for different reasons, except Agee hates himself more than Vollmann does. Agee feels he has no right to pry into the impoverished lives of the tenant farmers. Their welcoming shames him, and he tortures himself with thinking he cannot do anything for them, cannot help them, but only be an intruder into their lives. Agee's inability to fully empathize with them and to consider himself worthy of their love and friendship, his incredulity as to the possibility of establishing genuine human relationships with the wretched of the earth, bothers Vollmann. While trying to portray tenant families without fictionalizing or embellishing, Agee cannot entertain the idea that he might become a part of their lives: the division between them is inviolable. In contrast, Vollmann proceeds from the assumption that they are equals as human beings.

Such strong psychological undercurrents inevitably affect the execution. *Let Us Now Praise Famous Men* mostly reads like a manifesto of sorts on how to document raw experience without objectifying the people observed and encountered. The book proceeds hesitantly, insecurely, as Agee's worry over content shapes form: he meditates on the (im)possibility of conveying what he sees, hears, feels during the short, intimate time he spends with the three tenant families in Alabama. The book deviates from the conventions of reportage —the text digresses at every turn and spends more energy and time on what art and an artist can do than on the details of the lives of the tenant families. In other words, the book chronicles how Agee's encounter with the tenants is followed by the unsatisfactory attempt to write about them. This effort arrests the flow of the manuscript, turning it into Agee's confessions about his failure as an artist as well as a human being in the face of the radical other: the critical consensus is that *Let Us Now Praise Famous Men* reads mostly like an autobiography of sorts rather than a documentary work.

Similar worries permeate Vollmann's books: agonized meditations on how to do narrative justice to all the real people he has encountered is a constant worry for Vollmann. In *Poor People,* this anxiety turns into a classic instance of what Harold Bloom calls "the anxiety of influence" whereby an author commits literary patricide in order to assert the originality of his or her work: from the very first page, Vollmann tries to come to terms with Agee, part his inner demon, part his major influence. Vollmann takes Agee to task not merely for confessing his inadequacies but, more important, for denying the possibility of ever overcoming them. Agee fails at what Vollmann extols as the prime virtue of life and literature: true empathy. Where Agee fails, Steinbeck excels: in *Imperial,* which chronicles Vollmann's failed efforts at turning nonfiction into fiction, Vollmann turns to Steinbeck, who does not suffer from bouts of guilt as Agee does; Steinbeck is not paralyzed by extreme self-consciousness or guilt because he is capable of empathy. Agee, of privileged background, pities the suffering and the sufferer, unlike Steinbeck, who came from a disadvantaged background. In Vollmann's analysis, Agee is elitist, Steinbeck egalitarian. While Agee recoils in guilt at the sight of suffering and feels overwhelmed in the face of what he calls "essential human frailty, the ultimately mortal wound which is living and the indignant strength not to perish," Vollmann seems awed, almost attracted to it (*Famous,* 202). Vollmann chronicles his own writing failures, just as *Let Us Now Praise Famous Men* also does, but with a difference: Vollmann prefers to own up to his failures, to embrace them, and he turns his failures into a possibility for another form of self-expression—that of nonfiction without the self-pity Agee feels for himself as an artist, as a human being encountering the other. It may be the ending of *Poor People* that really establishes its difference from *Let Us Now Praise Famous Men:* the last two sections that address the paradoxes of the privileged trying to connect with the underprivileged and the possible problems with self-laceration. To what extent Vollmann manages to avoid Agee's faults is something he wants us to answer for ourselves.

Despite his passionate criticism of Agee, Vollmann embraces *Let Us Now Praise Famous Men*'s dictum that truth is nothing but experience itself and that in pursuit of truth literary reportage should attempt to record "unimagined existence" (8). Both writers are interested in the mundane lives of the underprivileged. In their treatment the mundane becomes sacred. Agee's goal is to record "human divinity," and Vollmann's profane chase of the divine, the spiritual, mimics that. Agee's feeling is more of a Christian love for the human, while Vollmann's secular sentiment is raw emotion, psychological need.

Last but not least, both Agee and Vollmann treat image and text as equal modalities. For Agee, they are "coequal, mutually independent, and fully cooperative." He insists that "if I could do it, I'd do no writing at all here. It would be photographs: the rest would be fragments of cloth, bits of cotton, lumps of earth, records of speech, pieces of wood and iron, phials of odors, plates of food and excrement" (13). A similar urge is evident in Vollmann, whose sketches in particular bring everyday objects into existence alongside his descriptions of the mundane aspects of life. Also, for Vollmann, images are inseparable from the tales he tells. He takes photographs of his subjects, who continue to live in his memory long after their brief encounters. He usually interlaces text with corresponding images, but in *Poor People* he appends them to the very end of the text. In *Let Us Now Praise Famous Men,* Evans's haunting photographs greet the reader in the front matter, and the lack of captions has a disorienting effect. Vollmann does the opposite in *Poor People* by ending the book with photographs of the people we have read about and identifying all 108 of them by name and location. We literally meet these people; we put faces to names, and perhaps more importantly, we put a face to poverty itself. The reader is prompted by parenthetical references to photographs that were taken during a given episode, but it is up to the reader to pause reading and flip to the pages the images are on or wait until reaching the end of the book to look at them. Since he includes the parenthetical indicators and because he wants these people engraved on our minds, the first approach seems to be the one he prefers. In addition, he also occasionally urges the reader to stop and go look at a picture. For instance, he suddenly prompts us to look at the photo of a little Filipino girl, wanting us to immediately share with him the penetrating gaze of that child looking at him behind the camera. She is looking at you, too, he says. There are other moments in which the illustrations help to make *Poor People* a more moving experience, as when we see the saintly calm on the scarred face of the crazy beggar girl Wan, or when we feel almost grateful that Sunee looks sober in the photos and is not clutching at imaginary things in the air and trying to strangle them, as Vollmann memorably describes her as doing when she was talking.

In contrast to *Poor People*, which urgently seeks to establish for itself a true precedent, *Imperial* (2009) seems confident in the model it follows and perfects. Agee is almost forgotten in this book, while Steinbeck is at its physical center, receiving abundant praise from Vollmann. At thirteen hundred pages, this is a mighty book that pursues a mighty theme, the textual sprawl charting the sprawling landscape of the southern border. It is no wonder that Vollmann calls it his *Moby-Dick*. It is a painstaking chronicle of the centuries-long history of Imperial County in California and the U.S.-Mexico border. With the zest of a historian and an ardent investigator, Vollmann delves into newspapers and many other documents from the 1900s onward housed in historical archives and brings to light details that rewrite a major part of the region's and nation's history. Immensely important, archival coverage is not the only strength of *Imperial*, however. Were it not for Vollmann's ingenious interviews with legal and illegal Mexican immigrants, his efforts to gain deeper understanding of these people's lives, aspirations, sufferings, and work conditions through absorbing every detail of every aspect of the Mexican-American border, his historical research would have been a mere backward glance. As a result of Vollmann's overarching perspective, however, the backward glance turns into a cautionary tale about the present and the future. The narrative crisscrosses many genres: revisionary history, journalism, documentary, ecocriticism, cultural and political critique, ethnographic study, memoir, and travel writing. Vollmann's comprehensive grasp of the essence of America might even have allowed him to produce, if he had so chosen, a magnificent novel, but the nonfictional form makes this grand endeavor more powerful than a fictional form would.

Vollmann became interested in the Imperial Valley in 1997 when his friend Larry McCaffery introduced him to the area. On his first visit, Imperial did not impress Vollmann. He found it "hot, flat, muted and dull. The badlands and mountains of San Diego appealed to me more; in the most objective sense, they offered entities to look at" (302). Over the years, Vollmann went to Imperial on writing assignments for magazines, and each visit presented him a new vista on the myriad forms of human suffering caused by border issues. The research widened, and slowly, *Imperial* came into being. Vollmann explains that at the onset of his research, he knew less, so he cared less. The only thing he was aware of was that Imperial country was once rich farmland with an abundant supply of water that somehow became California's poorest, driest place. Then he realized that the parable of John Steinbeck's *The Pearl* applied to Imperial, too: "When a poor man finds the pearl, everyone wants to get it from him. . . . The great wealth of Imperial, the pearl whose discovery revived her parched silt, was the water to which one accident of geography, a second of relative seniority, and a third of American water law's generosity . . . entitled her" (528).

Vollmann formulates this book as a revisionary history, a reevaluation of American myths. It is also a parable about an urgent global issue that does not have the large audience it deserves: water politics. The world is faced with diminishing water resources, and in the near future, the scarcity of water will give rise to the same controversies as the scarcity of other natural resources does. Water, in this parable, becomes the central agent in every conflict between the United States and Mexico. Actors claiming rights over the Imperial Valley's water, for just and unjust purposes, populate *Imperial*'s expansive history of a geography, and the psychological landscape Vollmann excavates is both real and imaginary.

We first need to unpack the meaning of Imperial for Vollmann. Imperial County lies on the California-Mexico border, where Mexicans try constantly and desperately to enter the United States illegally. Within the county, there is also a city called Imperial. The Imperial of the title, however, does not exist beyond this book or Vollmann's mind: he defines, in a sense, an undefined—and perhaps an ever undefinable—Imperial, an "amorphous region," possibly "an arbitrary, semi-imaginary area" (48, 110). Vollmann's Imperial seems to correlate to the region as it stood before 1848, when the "Treaty of Guadalupe Hidalgo cedes half of Mexico to U.S., including much of the area which I call Imperial" (1136). Hence, the region Vollmann calls Imperial is both Mexican Imperial and American Imperial: it suffers from a "maddening doubleness," a "bifurcation," unlike now, where it is made up of "mutually exclusive zones of authority" (185). In a section entitled "Definitions of Imperial" we read of the dichotomies that define it:

> Imperial is green, green fields, haystacks, and wide mountains. Imperial widens itself almost into boundlessness, like the Salton Sea as you go south. Imperial is bright fields, then desert wastes, stacks of hay bales almost Indian yellow. Imperial is a dark field glimmering white with irrigation sprays. Imperial is a loud lonely train whistling in darkness. Imperial dreams fragrant vegetable dreams. Imperial dreams resentfully of the wealth it could have if the stink of death would only depart from the broken-windowed resorts of the Salton Sea. Imperial is the smell of a feedlot on a hot summer night. . . . Imperial is the brown-skinned man who somehow missed every immigration amnesty and who now laments for the good old days of the 1950s when *all we needed back then was just a rancher to give a signature to back us up.* Imperial is solid white farmer-citizens, and the conglomerates who now own so many of them. . . . But most of all, Imperial is "Mexicans" legal and illegal, and Imperial is also "Mexican-Americans." . . . Legally and illegally they establish themselves upon the land, and they try to stay; they want to live. . . . *Imperial is the continuum between Mexico and America.* (49)

For Vollmann, all these attributes make Imperial "peculiar, enigmatic, sad, beautiful" (41). It was first a frontier for America and then an abandoned dream. As Vollmann puts it, "Imperial is a future of *Settlement, Organization, Progress, and Achievement,* which its own pioneers, settlers, and organizers might not like if they knew what was coming" (185). At the beginning of the twentieth century, this land was claimed, in an attempt to represent it as a symbol of American progress, to rank with the Nile Delta (116). But this representation was contradicted by the fact that irrigation was regulated by private enterprises, which also controlled the wealth of the landowners. The geographical promise of the region is thus a mere historical erratum. For Vollmann, understanding what Imperial is and what Imperial *was* is the main issue.

As usual with Vollmann books that include maps, figures, photographs, and sketches (most of which are Vollmann's own), *Imperial* opens with maps of the region hand drawn by him. Photographs he has taken are dispersed throughout the book. The first map, "The Entity Called Imperial" on page xxiv, signals Vollmann's approach to his subject matter in advance. In calling Imperial an "entity," Vollmann emphasizes how Imperial resists definitions and borders. Despite forming a border itself, it has a separate life, an independent existence that extends beyond borders; it is a state of mind, a historical plane unknown to official maps. It is the history of America, comprising its dreams and failures, beauties and cruelties.

This is evident in the opening page, which features a full-page 2002 reproduction of a 1924 Imperial County death certificate. The death certificate, which faces the dedication page, records the name of the deceased as "John Doe unknown Mexican" (x). For seventy-eight years, this person has remained unidentified. John Doe seems to acquire, in Imperial country, another dimension: he is an illegal immigrant who lives in the pages of *Imperial* and the county of Imperial. Vollmann dedicates his book to the memory of Serafin Ramirez Hernandez, "unknown, missing, illegal, Mexican," one among many that do not belong legally to the United States but do belong in some other mysterious way, perhaps because they represent "the entity called Imperial" and establish the contrast between the "American dream" and the "Mexican dream" (xi, 115). Seeking to understand the differences and similarities between these dreams amounts for Vollmann to an "attempt to become a better-informed citizen of North America": "Our 'American dream' is founded on the notion of the self-sufficient homestead. The 'Mexican dream' may be a trifle different, but requires its kindred material basis. Understanding how these two hopes played out over time required me to cultivate statistical parables about farm size, waterscapes, lettuce prices, et cetera. I have harvested them and now present them to you" (115).

The method Vollmann used to "harvest" information is one of the most important aspects of his endeavor in *Imperial*. Information resides in the human element, and Vollmann relies on it; in his interviews, he is not so much satisfying the stranger's need to learn by asking questions as engaging in an act of observing the answers manifest themselves in and through mundane circumstances. The time Vollmann spends with the people he interviews brings them closer, and he parts with many of them as friends. To illustrate, a day Vollmann spends with his new friend Lupe Vasquez, a migrant worker in the U.S. fields, helps him understand both this individual and the difference between the American and Mexican dreams. Vasquez, Vollmann learns, "who gets up at three-thirty to pick crops in and for another nation, is the difference between the right to happiness, which none of us can be guaranteed, and the right to happiness's pursuit, which I do find written into a certain early document of my United States" (262). This difference is manifested more concretely in the "two reifications of happiness, the self-sufficient American homestead and the Mexican *ejido*" (315). The contrast between these two means of farming constitute one of "the strange nuances of Imperial's history north and south: Mexican and American Imperial dream very different agrarian dreams." When homestead farmers arrived in the Imperial Valley, they dreamed of increasing self-sufficiency and independence on lands and "enlarged themselves beyond the statutory limits of the 1902 Reclamation Act" that allotted 160 and 320 acres of land, respectively, to single and family farms (327). In 1907, they were reminded that "the Reclamation Act forbade the delivery of water on any government project to privately owned lands to a greater extent than 160 acres" (327). Water expenses drove enlarged farms out of business, and they sold their land to powerful farming corporations. Small farms, in turn, failed to survive against the big corporate farms. Vollmann reports that by the 1920s "the ideal agrarian world was cashing out, bit by bit. . . . But the allure of the family farm only increased as it became more utopian" (334). By the 1930s and 1940s, the problem was even worse, and it gave rise to a new problem. Large farms, which were now an oppressive majority, were operated by "tenants," and many depended on "hired field labor" (572, 573). By 1945, less than half of Imperial County's workforce was practicing agriculture (574). Mexican field workers, who worked for very low wages, constituted the majority of those whose business was farming.

Mexican ejidos similarly suffered under government and corporate control. Ejidos, according to Vollmann, are "communal inalienable holdings, either from pre-Conquest times or else carved out of other lands by the Mexican Revolution" (xxix). The government owned these parcels of land, but as long as the farm was passed on from generation to generation for agricultural use, the family could "work" on and "bequeath" the land (335). In the first decade of the twentieth century, the U.S.-based Colorado River Land Company that provided irrigation services in Mexico bought—after much wrangling—many ejidos from the Mexican government. However, the cost of water was such that the company failed; after two decades, it went out of business and the farmers reclaimed their lands. Those ejodos still exist in small numbers; Vollmann notes that "in 2004, there were two hundred and twenty-eight *ejidos* in Baja California" (335). The American homestead, in contrast, has disappeared entirely. Vollmann argues there is a reason that ejidos "have not entirely failed to hold their own" (336): "In the *ejidos* somebody's farm might or might not get improved, and nobody else will give a damn. He might or might not make a success; he might spend the harvest season getting drunk with his mistress, and that is literally his affair. He has no intention of selling out, not ever; he is home" (340). The American homestead is the "mirror image" of the ejidos: whereas the American homestead failed in the face of farming corporations, the ejidos eventually freed themselves from them (336).

Turning to the present, Vollmann makes clear that the current state of affairs between the two sides of Imperial is one of constant struggle. *Imperial* opens with a typical scene from the present, as Vollmann observes U.S. border patrol agents on duty. Patrol agents keep their eyes on the All-American Canal that marks the border. Southside of the canal, "two Mexicans waited, not aliens yet; while on our side, Northside," an agent "sat calmly watching them in his car" (3). The scene is almost ordinary; it is one of the "methodical patrols and prowls to keep the have-not millions out of paradise—which in this case was Imperial County, California," the land where "fields of blondness, of endless pallid asparagus, onion plants like great lollipops and honey-colored hay bales produced the lowest median tax income of any county in the state" (3). The patrol is also a test of patience for the parties involved. Mexicans waited for hours on end to seize a chance to jump into the water of the canal, while the patrol agents waited for them to "pop their heads" out of the water (3). "Get out," the patrol agent shouts at the now-illegal Mexican, who heeds the directive but throws stones and curses as he disappears (4). The Mexican side of the river is "hot and thorny and dry," while on the other side are "all those American fields appearing so cruelly green like Paradise, because the water belongs to America" (6). Yet it is not America some people want to go to after they cross; rather, it is Canada, where they believe "you don't get hassled like you do in America" (6). For others, staying in an American prison and receiving basic shelter and food is also a good option. Vollmann learns that the average number of the deported varies per night, between eighty and six hundred Mexicans, most of whom are young and "agile" males capable of climbing the fence protecting the American border after swimming in the severely polluted, life-threatening water of the canal (13).

It may be difficult to cross the border, but it is definitely more difficult to stay alive in the desert surrounding Imperial. Mexican human smugglers, called coyotes, help illegal immigrants cross at exorbitant prices, increasing their chances of surviving on the desert and escaping the night-vision cameras of the patrol agents. Vollmann tries to talk to a coyote: "The coyote came out with his shoulders down like a charging bull. I nodded and smiled, but he looked at me with a strangely flat, almost watery gaze which I have long since learned signifies a gazer who cares not what evil he does, someone utterly and inhumanly unreachable. I saw this gaze once in a Russian paramilitary policeman during the Yugoslavian civil war; he soon held a bayonet to my throat to 'test' me. I saw it in some teenagers in Harlem who seared my arm with a cigarette butt" (26).

Evil naturally accompanies any human trafficking operation. The women smuggled by coyotes are raped as part of their crossing fee, and the women know this will happen beforehand, but in their desperation, this option seems like the lesser of two evils. Many coyotes abandon the crossers to die in the desert when border patrol catches them. In Vollmann's opinion, the financial arrangements of this trade are the worst cruelty the illegal immigrants suffer. Coyotes collect their fees when they deliver the crossers to their families or friends across the border, and it is almost always the family or friends that pay the coyote. In one way, this approach protects the crossers by preventing the coyote from "pocketing their money and murdering them" (31–32). However, the crossers become "merchandize" in the eyes of the coyote, who holds them in hotel rooms "until payment" (32). "These holding areas," Vollmann explains, can "be found in almost any town in Imperial County" (32). In case of delayed payments, the crossers become captives, and if nobody claims them, their fate remains unclear.

Another "consequence of the cash-on-delivery system" is that if the merchandise gets "lost in transit," the shipper sees "no reason to inform the recipient, who would now not be liable for payment." "To my mind," Vollmann states, this is "the most evil aspect of the trade" (32). Much worse is the fact that this is most likely to occur on U.S. territory. Hence the death certificate facing the dedication page, hence Serafin Ramirez Hernandez, who was in a coyote's van that caught fire, killing half of its sixteen passengers, all of whom were illegal border crossers. Vollmann learns about Hernandez via flyers his friends distribute on the street. The flyer has a photograph of the missing Hernandez, "whose blurred head," Vollmann thinks, "stared out at me from the flyer most distantly, resolutely seeking something beyond and behind me" (34). His file will remain open in the Mexican consulate in San Diego until his body is discovered. The frequency of such crossing tragedies is used by the U.S. authorities to warn and discourage illegal immigrants from working with coyotes. As Vollmann puts it, "My government had figured out that it could use deaths caused in part by its own policies to make propaganda" (38).

Nevertheless, neither illegal immigrants nor the border patrol officers are the real representatives of Imperial: water is, and has always been, the foremost actor in the history of Imperial. Indeed, nearly every entry in *Imperial*'s impressive "The Chronology of Imperial" registers a stage of Imperial's complicated history of water. The first entry to the chronology is dated "millions of years ago" and notes that the "Gulf of California reaches beyond the site of Indio," which is another county in California (1133). As the saying goes, where there is water there is life, and the next entry accordingly notifies us of the "first migration to Mexico" that reaches back to "as early as 40,000 BC." The water in question has a complex relationship with land, and as the third entry notes, while water receded toward the ocean, some of it accumulated in Salton Sink by 700 and gradually diminished over the next thousand years. In 1900, the prospect of irrigation heralded a miracle: what was desert until now would be turned into a paradise of farms and irrigation canals.

The same year a private enterprise called Imperial Land Company was established, which, in an effort to compensate for the U.S. government's lack of development in irrigation farming, supplied land leases and irrigation service to the farms the company sold. Their promise was that land is "like an inexhaustible bank account on which the plant life of the future may draw at will without danger of protest" (118). In 1901, the town of Imperial was founded. The same year, the Imperial Canal, later to be renamed the Alamo Canal, was built and irrigation began in the Imperial Valley (118). A newspaper's headline read: "Water in the town of Imperial: the headgates of the Imperial canal were opened: Water is here. The desert disappears" (119). The last two phrases become the ghosts that haunt the pages of *Imperial,* recurring throughout the book. By 1901, the Salton Sink was dry.

In 1902, the Reclamation Act created homestead programs for the Imperial Valley and allotted homesteads for single people and married couples (1140). By 1904, with the help of widespread private corporation propaganda about the "miracle of irrigation" that promised wealth and profit to the farmers of the Imperial Valley, the number of farmers and private water companies significantly increased. In 1904, mud and salt began building up in the Alamo Canal. Water companies of Imperial made "a cut in the Colorado River in Mexican territory for the New Imperial Canal," and a series of floods widened "this cut dangerously" (1141). In 1905, the flooding gave rise to the New River (called the Río Nuevo in Baja) and formed the Salton Sea, or as Vollmann puts it, the Salton Sea "flooded itself into being" (1141, 50). In 1907, Imperial became a county. Between 1910 and 1920, Imperial County ranked as "the third-fastest-growing county in the U.S," during which time the valley was inhabited by half of the total population of California (1141).

As this brief history demonstrates, water came to Imperial Valley unnaturally and brought with it long-term complications. The irrigation system did not last very long due to salination and alkalinization, as is usual with irrigation systems. The polluted waters flowed into the Salton Sea, which gradually acquired its terrible smell and poisonous water that otherwise supported the region's avian and fish population. Vollmann reports that the Salton Sea is currently populated by "half-mummified birds and fishes crunching underfoot" either because the water is "poisonous" or excessively "salty" (42).

Imperial guides us through unknown, ignored histories, facts, and human sufferings, revealing a past that is necessary to answering the question of how we should live, for "without a past, no matter how controvertible, the present cannot be anything other than a tumble through darkness towards the darkness which neither past nor present can illuminate" (42). Vollmann's methodology is grounded in an acceptance of Imperial's mysteries: "Imperial is a place I'll never know, a place of other souls than mine; and how can anyone know otherness?—Through study, perhaps; through history" (114). Part of the history of the region is told through the propaganda that was used to encourage settlement in Imperial. For instance, Vollmann paraphrases a newspaper ad in 1903 that insisted there was no place elsewhere in the arid West where "so large a tract of so fertile soil, capable of being furnished with a water supply so abundant at so low a price for the water right and with so cheap water for all time to come" could be found (123). Vollmann thinks that the miracle-like representation of water in Imperial was a denial of the finite or of the concept of finitude that is emblematic of the American national character: "Yes, the Colorado River can burst through the cut, sweep away Mexicali, and scour a deep gorge for the Río Nuevo to speed through, but someday that gorge will go dry; in fact, it already has; the Río Nuevo's foul black spew is dead and buried" (119). Still, it is this willful ignorance of the finite source of water that created Imperial. As Vollmann puts it, "water is life; Imperial is, among other things, water; we are Americans, so water must be infinite" (123). The epigraph to the book quotes from the 1909 Yearbook of the United States Department of Agriculture: "As long as a farmer has an abundance of water, he almost invariably yields to the temptation to use it freely, even though he gets no increased returns as a result" (ix). To elaborate on the American yearning for the infinite, Vollmann reads Emerson's words in "The Young American" (1844) as a "hymn to possession": "The bountiful continent is ours, state on state, and territory on territory, to the waves of the Pacific sea" (qtd. in *Imperial,* 119). Vollmann interprets this line as implying that for Emerson "the days and lands" of his life "remain literally innumerable" (119). He then quotes the remarks of a senatorial candidate in 1898, who reminded Americans of things to be accomplished: there were "canals to be dug, railways to be laid, forests to be felled, cities to be built, unviolated fields to be tilled, priceless markets to be won, ships to be launched, peoples to be saved, civilization to be proclaimed, and the flag of liberty flung to the eager air of every sea" (qtd. in *Imperial,* 120). Vollmann exclaims in a similar spirit, "We peeled half of Mexico, now we're off to Spanish Cuba! Our soon-to-be-Senator elects *us* the chosen people. . . . And in the first decade of the twenty-first century, the most self-confident American President ever proclaims civilization in Iraq and Afghanistan—mission accomplished!" (120).

In Vollmann's opinion, all these instances of progress, of mission accomplished, are exemplified in the conflict over water that began as early as 1848 with the Treaty of Guadalupe Hidalgo, which established the Mexican-American border by drawing imaginary coordinates between the rivers Mexico and the U.S. share. Until 1942, when the All-American Canal was completed, however, the border lacked the oppressive force it has now. Once the All-American Canal was built, Vollmann explains, "the ecological, economic, and moral effects of the [border] line" became "ever more hurtful" to the south side of Imperial (246). For instance, in mid-1980s, completely devoid of the water sources it had once received naturally, Mexico desperately collected the seeping water from the canal to irrigate its farms. In response, the United States insisted that the seepage belonged to it; that it reserved the right "to lay concrete" that would prevent its water "from crossing without permission to Southside" (931). After the lining of the canal in 2003, Mexico, which was relying on the seepage and lacked alternative sources for irrigation, filed suit against the United States. By then, however, the water of the river was excessively salty, and saline water is not good for farming. Vollmann comments, "the rest of southern California might be thirsty and thirstier for Colorado River water, but you know what? American Imperial (we'll ignore her Mexican sister) had been here first! Other water districts are, in the Imperial Irrigation District's considered legal opinion, *junior rightholders*" (923–24).

The strife over water is not limited to agricultural use and, surprisingly, not merely a matter of international dispute. Imperial's water is also needed to meet the demands of nearby cities. "As the millennium turned," Vollmann explains, "Imperial's eponymous county got squeezed by San Diego, Los Angeles. . . . *The Urbans,* as Imperial County called them, requested her to sign a water-transfer agreement which would begin to dry up the farms in whose name she had come into being" (930). Yet a century ago, Imperial asked the world, "You want your broccoli year-round, don't you? . . . And you want it at a low price, right? Well, then no reductions in water deliveries for us, please, not ever!" (925). During the 1990s, water companies under the guise of farm companies redirected the irrigation water of the Imperial Valley through pipelines to counties like San Diego and further diminished its agriculture (926–27). For Vollmann, although this phenomenon may seem recent, Imperial has always been about water farmers rather than agriculture farmers (927). Wittily, Vollmann wonders, "Is the Imperial on the north side of the international line American or un-American, and what does the answer to that question say about what Americans profess?" (159). Perhaps Vollmann is right in thinking of Imperial as the undivided space between the south and north of Imperial Valley: they seem one when it comes to the water they have lost.

Although Vollmann initially planned to make *Imperial* a historical novel, he ultimately chose to write a work of nonfiction instead, and he defends this decision with a well thought-out argument that seems significant in at least two senses. First, it clarifies Vollmann's ideas on the novel as a genre. Second, Vollmann explains his approach to nonfiction as the presentation of real life.

Vollmann explains that his "original intent was to write a novel about Imperial, a story which followed the lives of [illegal immigrants] from Southside all the way across the wall and desert to, say, Yuma, where they labored for low wages until they got caught and deported" (163). Toward that end, he wrote six tentative beginning chapters that appear in *Imperial*. Each time Vollmann attempted to fictionalize Imperial and make it cohere and take the shape of a novel, his efforts were thwarted: he turned back to his memories and rewrote anecdotes from his experiences that he narrates in *Imperial* and ends abruptly. But despite choosing a nonfiction genre for *Imperial*, he maintains that we all write fiction out of what we observe. "We all do it," Vollmann claims, "we're all novelists" (163). He seems to mean that imagination is at work in the interpretation of most mundane events, let alone historical events. The tentative beginnings of the unwritten novel of Imperial can thus be said to reveal Vollmann's imagination trying to understand, interpret his experiences.

Nevertheless, he did not end up writing a novel about Imperial for reasons that seem to question the worth or reliability of a novelistic representation of this particular topic, a topic he believed he had not yet mastered. He illustrates this point by referring to a Mexican woman named Maria whose life he observed. She was a teacher in Mexico but worked as an illegal laborer, a housecleaner, in Sacramento, California. She had a brother who worked as an accountant in Mexico, and he helped her with cleaning whenever he visited. If, by chance, the brother ran into the owner of the house, he'd "rush to show his picture identification," his expression "pitiable beyond abject: it must be a reflex, the reflex of submission to this foreign power which took half his country but which repays the theft by oozing money from its bowels—what phrase could better locate his sister who cleans toilets?" (170). Maria's life could be the subject of a novel, yet Vollmann doubts whether he can truly know Maria or "learn enough about Maria's life to express the respect I have for her endurance, and the compassion I feel for her intellect which wastes itself on drudgery" (170). In this sense, fictionalizing a real person's plight is also an act of "pay[ing] tribute," and it is definitely different from "invent[ing] a character" (170). Vollmann concludes that he does "not understand enough about border people to describe them without reference to specific individuals"; he "remains too ill acquainted with them to fictionalize them" (170). Witnessing the hardships that shape the life of a person does not necessarily mean knowing that person completely. By the same token, he does not deny the possibility of establishing intimacy with these strangers in a way that allows them to be friends. In other words, once the acquaintance was well established, he could perhaps invent stories. Until then, however, "making up tales about Maria's life would not only be disrespectful to her, it would be bad art. . . . The best compliment I can pay Maria is that I cannot imagine her life, especially the drudgery of it but also its various helplessnesses, humiliations, and apprehensions. . . . Someday, if I ever get out into the world and see more, suffer more, which might not be worth it, writing a novel about her might be an act of beauty and truth" (170).

Although Vollmann emphasizes the necessity of a deeper understanding of people's suffering as the prerequisite of a fictional account of reality, it is not in his view sufficient. He insists that a novel about Maria's miserable life "would have failed, because respect must encompass more than the heroine's victimhood. It needs also to embrace her various happinesses and her silliness about parrots" (173). In other words, the novelist has to take into account (or imagine) every tragedy, joy, folly, and anything and everything else that makes a character fully and truly human. Vollmann develops this idea with reference to Gustave Flaubert's story "A Simple Heart," in which Felicité, a devoted maid-servant who spends her life in drudgery, is depicted as a dim-witted person that builds her life around harmless but foolish passions. It is Flaubert's overt portrayal of Felicité's "stupidity" that makes the story a "masterpiece"; Flaubert makes us "realize that of all the characters in this story, she's by far the finest, a fact never noticed by any of the busy, self-absorbed human beings around her" (171). This realization constitutes an epiphany for Vollmann: "What 'A Simple Heart' did for *my* heart when I first read it many years ago was to alert me to the probability that among the people whom I myself overlooked, there might be Felicités, whose hidden goodness would do *me* good to find her. Later, when I began writing books, it occurred to me that discovering and describing those goodnesses might accomplish some external good, perhaps even to Maria and Felicité, who have less need of our pity than we might think. Suppose that [Felicité's mistress], after reading my version of 'A Simple Heart,' refrained just once from assaulting Felicité with harsh words. Or is that aspiration ridiculous?" (171).

We may perhaps know whether or not it is ridiculous by looking at one of the tentative beginnings of the unwritten novel version of Imperial and decide for ourselves. The beginning adapts the first paragraph of "A Simple Heart" and credits Flaubert as the author. The mistress-servant relationship turns into an employer-employee relationship in a Mexican factory (*maquiladora*) where women stoically endure sexual abuse so that they can keep receiving pathetic sums of wages for backbreaking work (172). In other words, it is a modern-day master-slave story, and it is one that demonstrates that victimhood has no bounds: the factory is owned by Americans and it is located on nontillable land in Mexico, whose farms dried up when the water of the Colorado was denied to them. For these women working in factories, challenging abuse is a reason for immediate termination, which would likely mean starvation, since these factories are the only options for many that cannot go to the United States, legally or illegally, to work for even lower wages. Vollmann decides that it is not easy to justify using stories that detail such brutality in works of art. "And yet of course it *would* be right to make a poem or a song, a painting or a novel about it," Vollmann clarifies, "if doing so would help anyone to *feel*. Steinbeck might have been able to do it. Maybe someday I will attempt to do it. At the moment, I cannot presume to do anything with this story except to show it to you, tiptoe around it, and walk away" (174). Of course, by "tiptoe," Vollmann underestimates the richness of his descriptions of these factories, the forceful simplicity and heartbreakingly enlightening aspects of his conversations with the workers, and the power of the seemingly subjective yet factual narrative he offers on the disturbing conditions of the factories. Therefore, when he walks away, the reader does not experience pathos but is rather left throbbing with pain and anger, if not sadness.

John Steinbeck looms large behind Vollmann's realized and abandoned endeavors in writing *Imperial*. Another tentative beginning for the unwritten novel is credited to Steinbeck: "Maria loved truth and hated untruth" (178). Steinbeck said something similar about his friend Ed Ricketts after he died: "The man 'loved what was true and hated what wasn't'" (178). "I feel protective toward this dead writer," Vollmann states (175). "Steinbeck desired all of us to be angry and sorry about the plight of the Okies, and his own outrage makes *The Grapes of Wrath* a great book" (177). What is even greater is Steinbeck's "distrust of authority" in the face of the American national trust in government, which makes him "one of the most un-American Americans of his time" (177). "I want to be un-American like him," Vollmann asserts, "unaffiliated with anything but balance. I want to show Felicité's goodness and stupidity together" (177). His praise of his favorite novel by Steinbeck, *East of Eden* (1952), may also be read as a defense of, if not guidance for, his own writing: "If Steinbeck occasionally mistook sentimentality for truth, well, there remain worse vices. Steinbeck worried and at times grew bitter, but he was never cynical. One aspect of his credo which too many of us misperceive as sentimental is his very imperial glorification of individual choice. If I dislike, say, what America 'stands for,' and if I express that feeling in public, I may find that certain other Americans dislike *me*. That happened to Steinbeck. The many bannings of *The Grapes of Wrath* comprise its badge of honor. This book upset people. It actually had something to say. It was angry, unashamedly sexual and un-American. Being un-American, Steinbeck was the most American of us all" (178).

Imperial does not pretend to be *The Grapes of Wrath* for Imperial, but it follows a similar methodology by offering a sociological analysis of the region. In Vollmann's opinion, there is a difference between collecting information and planting it in a narrative in an organized manner. *Imperial* grapples with the question of writing sociology and collecting facts. In not fictionalizing these facts, Vollmann aims to achieve an effect that a novel might not: he provides reality in its unadorned, simple form. For instance, referring to the hundreds of people with whom he has acquainted himself Vollmann notes, "I would never consider changing a word of their stories. They are real and they have taught me many things that are true as I peer into the mystery called Mexico" (180). As he explains, "It is they, the Mexicans and Mexican-Americans, the cabbage-pickers legal and illegal, whom it is slowly becoming my privilege to know. Imperial is what I want it to be, but they are ones who are what they are. The desert is real, as are they, but there is no such place as Imperial" (181). Nonetheless, the book does an excellent job of bringing it into existence, with the hesitations Agee has taught Vollmann to avoid and embrace at the same time.

CHAPTER 5

Rising Up and Rising Down: Some Thoughts on Violence, Freedom and Urgent Means

Rising Up and Rising Down: Some Thoughts on Violence, Freedom and Urgent Means may be the most ambitious work in Vollmann's body of writing. The purpose of this three-thousand page, seven-volume magnum opus, which was more than two decades in the making, is to answer a simple question: when is violence justified? He traveled around the world to investigate contemporary acts of violence and read world history extensively with an eye to violent behavior. The manuscript was complete by 1998 but it was not published until 2003, when Dave Eggers heard of the project and its troubles of finding a publisher. *Rising Up and Rising Down* came out from McSweeney's in a handsome, limited number slip-case set that was never reprinted. The book was a finalist for the National Book Critics Circle Award in 2003. Vollmann cut three-quarters of the original text and Ecco, an imprint of HarperCollins, published the more accessible abridged edition in 2005.[1] In a letter to his literary agent, Vollmann explains that *Rising Up and Rising Down* is "my life's work" and it "attempts to delineate a moral calculus for violence. . . . I believe this is one of the most important tasks which the human mind can hope to undertake. We read the Bible, Aquinas, Thucydides, Marx, Hitler, Gandhi, Caesar, and so many others" to help form our opinions on this question among others (*Expelled from Eden*, 327, 325).

In humility, Vollmann acknowledges the possible flaws of his endeavor because he does not have any formal training in philosophy or logic. Nonetheless, he asserts that *Rising Up and Rising Down* derives from his readings and travels, and refrains from being confounding, so he considers it accessible to anyone with an interest in understanding violence. To the extent that his claims that "the subject of ethical violence remains largely unexplored" and that he does not "know of any comparable work" are true, his belief about the importance of his book would seem to be well grounded (327). It could, Vollmann claims, be "used in classes in: ethics, history, philosophy, criminology, Slavic studies, Asian studies, political science, and perhaps military science." Yet its length made it difficult to find a publisher.

The title's *rising up,* refers, as Vollmann explains, to "a just act of violence. Both ends and means are legitimate," and *rising down,* refers to "an unjust act of violence. Means, ends, or both fail to meet legitimacy's standard" (*Rising* 453). Despite the fact the Vollmann believes there is such a thing as justified war, a general sense of discomfort with excuses offered to legitimize violence pervades the book. What is most vexing about violence, in other words is that whether it takes the form of acts of terror, self-defense, or military or police activity, it is always accompanied by a series of justifications, just or unjust, of defense: defense of class, defense of ideology, defense of honor, defense of ground, defense of authority. Vollmann, not content with many of these justifications, hopes "to arrive at a way of ethically categorizing violence" (45).

The biggest challenge in this ethically motivated task is the fact that violence is usually justified with "moral values" that either absolutize or relativize its excuses (xi). Vollmann holds that "every violent act refers itself back to some more or less rational explanation that may succumb to relativism. For instance, violence may be justified on the basis of "defense of homeland," but another justification of violence, such as "defense of authority," may invalidate it (xii). What happened in Yugoslavia during the civil war between Serbs and Croatians in the 1990s is a case in point: "authority's federalism, which just happens to have a Serbian flavor, mobilizes its defensive violence against Croatian defense of ethnicity and localism. Here is where relativism comes in." In such circumstances, how can we decide whose defense, and therefore violence, is right and necessary? Vollmann's purpose in this book is to give these questions their ethical due.

The hefty material of *Rising Up and Rising Down* is divided neatly into two parts, "Categories and Justifications," which includes volumes 1 through 4, and "Studies in Consequences," which includes volumes 5 and 6. The seventh volume is titled "The Moral Calculus," volume MC. Vollmann explains that "although this volume is stored against the left-hand edge of the slipcase, it is not necessarily intended to be read first. Instead, it should serve as a 'resource volume,' to be referred to whenever useful" (*Rising,* volume MC, 11). Vollmann includes "The Moral Calculus" in its entirety in the abridged edition and places it at the heart of the book by inserting it between parts 1 and 2. Vollmann also offers an annotated table of contents to the unabridged edition so that the full complexity of the series is not lost on the reader reading the compact edition.

In the first part Vollmann discusses, providing examples and deliberately inconclusive arguments, when violent defense of honor, class, authority, and ground is justified and when it is not. He studies for example, how Gandhi's actions accord with the prescriptions of the Golden Rule, how Napoleon's stack up against the limits and requirements of collective and individual honor during wartime, and how Stalin's line up with his socialism. He tries to filter the particular justification for violence or nonviolence in each example through "induction and common sense" and explains that his "intention was neither to uncover new facts about the doings of historical figures, nor to formulate new interpretations of them" (45). Instead what he was trying to do was "to lay out the received wisdom . . . and then judge that" (45–46).

Although Vollmann offers ethical judgments on possible justifications for given acts of violence, he refrains from presenting those judgments as absolute. A major purpose of *Rising Up and Rising Down,* in fact, is to urge the reader to rely on empathy to make his or her own decisions. As Vollmann puts it, "The reader is invited to consider each of the moral decisions undertaken by our historical protagonists as the centerpiece of a parable" and see whether he or she can imagine himself or herself into these circumstances (46). In fact, he seems to envision a kind of correspondence with the reader; believing that his subject matter is of great concern to ethical human life, Vollmann enthusiastically shares his thoughts with the reader. In his preface to the abridged edition, he addresses his readers: "Thank you for reading this book. My sincere intention in writing it was to be helpful" (xiii). Likewise, in the preface to the seven-volume original edition, he writes, "I offer it to you, my unknown reader, in the hope that it may someday save a life or comfort a seeking mind" (xv). His appeal to the participation of the reader is one of the biggest assets of his book in its explicit demand for a more ethical consideration of violence: "The suffering of others shames me and awes me," and "if we think about a sufficient number of cases we may be able to plant the seeds of a tentative ethics which others could consider, pick and choose from and hopefully benefit from even if they cannot improve" (31).

We can look at "The Moral Calculus" as a condensed version, in the mode of a chart or an outline, that lists the questions that the parables raise and the tentative answers, or maxims, Vollmann formulates for them. Vollmann arrives at the "principles of conduct" his calculus suggests after extracting moral codes from his "theoretical" studies in the first part (445). Yet he refrains from declaring that these principles are universally true: "Should you find fault with the calculus, as you ought to do (I do my best to find fault with everybody else's; and my chapter on defense of animals remains especially unsatisfactory), I respectfully ask you not to leave a vacuum, but to construct your own" (445). The first entry in "The Moral Calculus," entitled "What is the Best Way to Seek the Truth," reiterates this point and serves as a methodical guide to the whole endeavor itself, offering maxims and then corollaries, examples, and caveats for each proposal. In the abridged edition, Vollmann deploys "The Moral Calculus" as a bridge connecting the first part's investigations to the final part's extensively researched and detailed ethical evaluations of major events of recent violence; it also offers convenient access to the delineation of the just and unjust moral values surrounding justifications of violence.

The prefaces to both editions of *Rising Up and Rising Down* help us situate the project in a historical and cultural as well as philosophical and literary context. While the one composed for the abridged edition reads more like a description of the project, the preface to the unabridged edition reflects the many decades Vollmann spent working on the book. In a brief paragraph, Vollmann defines his project as an "essay" and posits it "as a companion piece to my memoir *An Afghanistan Picture Show* and to my novel *You Bright and Risen Angels*" because these works, like *Rising Up and Rising Down*, engage with a "do-it-yourself politics of an extreme character" (xv). This sense of continuity in subject matter and critical approach attests to Vollmann's wide-ranging, all-encompassing preoccupation with issues he finds important.

The not-so-subtle critique in the supplementary paragraph of the preface depends as much on Vollmann's personal judgments as on his growing comprehension of human nature and its propensity for cruelty and self-righteousness while he worked on his meditation on violence. He explains that over the two decades of the making of his book he discovered "a lack of decency and compassion" in people's personal moral values (143). This is partly due to the fact that "most of us expediently rig our own moral calculuses in such a way that our actions become automatically justified in accordance with our own urgencies" (141). Also, since violence is imprinted in our DNA, we can only hope to "prevent" future ones through an ethical study of acts of violence (41):

> Induction leads to the conclusion that human behavior winds on morally unaltered, and probably unalterable. "Now earth was corrupt in God's sight," says the book of Genesis, "and the earth was filled with violence. And God saw the earth, and behold, it was corrupt; for all flesh had corrupted their way upon the earth." If violence is a kind of dust that lies inside the house of the soul, there does not seem to be any way to sweep it out the door. We can only sweep it into one corner or another. Go back fifty

> thousand years to the Neanderthal man whom archeologists would find "frontally stabbed in the chest by a right-handed antagonist." To murder is not only human, but protohuman. . . . As that Neanderthal homicide proved, human violence itself cannot be altered without altering human nature. "Vice and virtue form the destinies of the earth," said Robespierre; and on the day that that is no longer true, there will be no more human beings as we understand them. (23–25)

Far from being deterministic, Vollmann believes that by becoming responsibly and critically aware, we can discover what the true meaningful, just, responsible human life amounts to. He insists that we should "grant our authority as human beings, as citizens, to judge each other's means, even when those means do not directly affect the rights of our sovereign private selves" (117). Hence, his preoccupation with ethics, which he claims has been frequently deployed as a "metaphor" by "revolutionaries, conquerors, patriots, and the other violent movers" (117). Instead, ethics should guide us in "the evaluations of justifications" in which violence is normalized on improbable bases (118).

Nonetheless, discourses on human progress may seem to contribute to the normalization, if not to the camouflage, of violence. "Yes, we now have 'laws of war'" Vollmann admits, "but we inhabit a planet in which the commission of atrocities remains normal" (22). He disputes the widespread argument that violence on global, local, and tribal scales "no longer stains our planet":

> Which outrages upon freedom, safety, and peace vanished? Rape, murder, torture, slavery and compulsion, censorship, war and institutionalized tyranny—the marks of all these I've seen with my own eyes. To be sure, the *forms* of them do vary, and so do their relative proportions and frequencies. Human sacrifice, for instance, is at present much less common than assassination and genocide as expressions of religious praxis. Violence no longer hovers over the ballot box in American cities; it's in other lands. Institutionalized slavery is neither as widespread nor as overt as it was two hundred years ago, although it can still be found in the Sudan, Thailand, Cambodia, the Philippines, and doubtless a hundred other habitats for sweatshops, forced prostitution, and indentured servitude. . . . Torture, now in its renaissance, is committed by a third of all the governments on this earth. . . . The telling fact is the sameness of the calamities we inflict upon one another. (Yes, the forms change; the shapes of the wounds change.) (22)

Although "we need not delude ourselves that 'history' has accomplished much in the way of human improvement," human history is not static, and we can learn from differences across time: "The world was different once. Learn what today's truth has in common with yesterday's. Hitler invokes defense of homeland. So does Lycurgus the Spartan" (22, 447). Interestingly, "my President [George W. Bush] invokes it today. Which of those two predecessors, if either, does he more faithfully resemble?" (447).

In a sense, Vollmann finds optimistic reassurances of peace unsound, insincere, and manipulative. For instance, in response to a military historian's claim that "despite the confusion and uncertainty, it seems just possible to glimpse the emerging outlines of a world without war," Vollmann declares, "Maybe so —if thermonuclear war exterminates all of us" (49). Vollmann is not a cynic; rather, he simply thinks it is important to frequently underline the fact that human violence will exist as long as the human species continues to exist without giving up on the possibility of and responsibility of doing something for the world: "Putting aside any notion that the world is becoming a better place was neither easy not pleasant for me; and I've not yet given up believing both that the world *ought* to be better and that we have a duty to construct methods of improvement" (21). At the same time, he admits that our powers are limited: "Isolationism, greed, anger, fear, ethnic nationalism, racial and class hatred, murderous coldheartedness and native human viciousness, once called original sin, now more politely known as the aggressive propensity, continue to narrow justice" (21).

At the beginning of *Rising Up and Rising Down,* Vollmann undertakes a philosophical meditation on death and by extension the meaning of life. For him, the compelling force of violence on human thought is its inherent connection to death. "Death is ordinary," Vollmann asserts. "Behold it, subtract its patterns and lessons from those of the death that weapons bring, and maybe the residue will show what violence is" (1). During an excursion, Vollmann walks through the Paris catacombs, which "organized death's jetsam according to a sanitary aesthetics— . . . joints of bones, heads of bones, promiscuously touching, darkness in the center of each" (1). The catacombs contain "the remains of about six million persons—our usual number of Jews who died in the Holocaust" (2). He finds the coincidence interesting because "the crimes which the Nazis accomplished with immense effort in half a dozen years, nature had done here without effort or recourse and was doing" (2). His preoccupation with the ordinariness of death, however, is shadowed by the senselessness of all deaths, either by violence or not. For Vollmann death is a form of self-understanding, of "self-knowledge," that we try to ignore because it hurts (5). Refusing to see dead bodies is, in his view, refusing to acknowledge the inevitable future status of our own bodies. Acceptance of the inevitability of death is analogous to the unpleasant recognition of one's greed, selfishness, or cruelty after a rigorous and honest self-investigation. When death, which we push out of our consciousness at every chance, forces itself on us by way of others' deaths, it hurts because we not only have failed to evade it but also have to make sense of it. There are, of course, various ways of granting meaning to death, justification of violence aside. Vollmann notes, for instance, a former pediatric oncologist who leaves his practice because he is only able to save 25 percent of the terminally ill children he treats, and the emotional damage this causes has taken its toll (11). Yet while he fails to accept and understand death as an oncologist, he finds comfort working in his new job as a coroner: investigating dead bodies for causes of death of all kinds (murder, suicide, violent accidents, natural causes) through all kinds of dissections and mutilations, the former oncologist comes to "understand a dead man" (10). When the cause of death materializes as a biological fact or criminal act or an accident, death becomes comprehensible.

This seems to hold true as long as one is privileged—or shall we say blessed—by a personal disaffiliation, especially in the case of death that comes through violence. The former pediatric oncologist may manage to evade death's mutilation of his heart and soul by dissociating himself from his terminally ill child patients, but a Serbian woman who loses her fiancé to violent death under Croatian attack becomes another victim to that same violence. Her all-encompassing hatred, her maddening incomprehension, leads her to attach a face to the "Angel of Death," the face of the opponent, the oppressor, the whole ethnic group, the whole nation, and the whole race (18, 19). When death acquires a face through violence, the human heart is irrevocably mutilated. This pains Vollmann.

The conclusion Vollmann comes to as to why killing is justified during times of war but prohibited during times of peace is that "a major ethical constituent of violence is *the unique relationship between each victim and perpetrator at a given time*" (38). This gives rise to a problem, namely, that "if the motive and context are so crucial, then we must ask whether one can with equal justification kill out of hatred, out of fear, out of rational self-defense or out of mercy" (38). The case of the Holocaust, however, invalidates this uniqueness principle. With respect to violent acts on massive scales, Vollmann argues, "the individuality of victims and perpetrators remains immaterial to our judgment: by their very large numbers, the dead in that pit constitute a silent scream of crime. We know all we need to know (except, of course, how to stop it next time)" (41). The crime is one "against humanity because it attack[s] human diversity, without which the whole concept of humanity becomes reduced to ethnicity or nationality" (39–40).

Another forceful argument Vollmann makes regards "the morality of weapons" (59). A weapon grants its owner "the three gods of violence": "security, autonomy, and power" (59, 53). What is willfully ignored, for Vollmann, is the fact that "a gun in my hand prepares me, transforms me. If I can accurately shoot paper targets from a distance today, I have a better chance of being able to shoot my enemies tomorrow" (53). This is called the "law of might," which "accords respect to an armed individual, who may well come to respect himself accordingly" (53). Vollmann finds a fatal danger in this law: "The capacity to do violence extends the self: it does not only arm it, it also 'hands' it, awarding it extra fingers of choice. The weapon becomes a limb, a friend" (55). In the United States, gun ownership gains another dimension: it becomes an instrument of the national creed of self-reliance (662). "The price we pay," Vollmann argues, "is one Columbine massacre after another. What some of us get in exchange, or at least what we strive for, is a sense of wholeness, pride, fulfillment best known to the hunter-gatherer. In the hands of a Columbian *para,* a gun is primarily a tool of terror, deterrence, retribution, revenge. . . . For an American, for better or worse, [it is] an 'equalizer.' . . . Self-reliance equals defiance. . . . Americans solve their own problems. . . . That is why . . . those two despised boys at Columbine brought guns to school and solved their own problems, evilly and uselessly" (662–63).

For an ethical evaluation of its rights of self-defense, however, the self should begin with the right to make choices regarding ethical decisions leading up to violent or nonviolent self-defense. The choices available to a victim of aggressive bullying behavior illustrate this point nicely. The victim may choose to show nonviolent resistance to bullying acts. This passivity, however, cannot be justified because neither the violence nor the nonviolent resistance serves a particular faith or ideology (76). Such passive self-defense can typically only be justified "in extreme situations" in which martyrs endure violence for a cause (75). Further, countering violence with nonviolence may only lead the victim to "become an unwitting accomplice in [the bully's] sadism" (76); as in most cases of violence, such as rape, infanticide, and murder, "the victims seem to be mere placeholders, almost accidental outlets. Violence rises up and takes the sacrifices it finds. It employs the means that it finds. It even takes whatever motives it finds" (28).

Like defenses of the use of violence in "nonsociopathic homicides," defenses of the use of violence in upholding honor and maintaining class distinctions are also problematic. Honor has both inward and outward aspects and is both collective and individual (151). Appealed to at times of conflict to unite ethnic or racial groups and nations, collective honor overrides the consciences of individuals. However, "collective honor ought never to be its own justification. True honor, the only kind whose defense is justifiable, is that which allows one to evaluate the goodness of an end, and to make a judgment as to the ethical suitability of a means to an end. This is the honor that keeps one from becoming a rapist or executing unarmed prisoners of war, that tells when the time has come to kill and die in defense of one's country" (159).

CHAPTER 6

Europe Central

2005 National Book Award winner *Europe Central* retells the disasters of World War II in a compelling blend of fact and fiction. In a novel comprising thirty-seven interlinked stories, Vollmann chronicles the ill-fated lives of several historical and imaginary characters from the Eastern front of the war. With his usual distrust of authority, he explores the deceptions and self-destruction of two totalitarian ideologies, Soviet communism and Nazi fascism. Vollmann proceeds from "the moral equation of Stalinism and Hitlerism" and dismisses the official American take on World War II as the "good war" (754).[1] His purpose is not to reiterate the evils of these totalitarian ideologies; it is a given that these ideologies are morally bankrupt. He is not trying to find the good, either, for that would be reductive, if not impossible. Vollmann instead attempts to imagine and represent the ways in which such evil shapes human lives and questions whether individuals have the capacity to make and remake their moral compasses, the willpower to redefine the morally right *and* wrong for themselves outside ideological confines.

Such issues have always preoccupied Vollmann, but with *Europe Central,* the stakes seem higher. In an interview, he talks about "the deeper truth" that he probes in this book, namely, the prospect that "if I were born in that time and place, I probably would've been one [a communist or a fascist]. And even if I resisted with all my being, I would still have characteristics of one, no matter what I did" (Dushane, 2).While his empath's sentiment makes him think he could easily have been a Nazi, his German ancestry makes him feel personally responsible for Nazi atrocities.[2] This is commendable honesty, but it does not explain his intentions in *Europe Central;* the book is too wide in its reach to be reduced to an effort at slaying inner demons. It would be more productive to treat the book as another example of Vollmann's constant thinking about moral dilemmas. It is similar to his life's work, *Rising Up and Rising Down,* as it constitutes "a series of parables about famous, infamous and anonymous European moral actors at moments of decision" (753).[3] Instead of focusing on the German side only, he treats World War II as a collective failure of ideologies. To that end, he presents us with psychological portraits not only of perpetrators but also of victims from the Soviet and German camps. He places them in challenging situations and watches them as they confront dilemmas: we descend, along with Vollmann, to the darkest recesses of the human heart and witness the heroic efforts of individuals to find the morally right thing to do in their respective circumstances and the pathetic and wicked acts of those who either fail at or give up on that endeavor. *Europe Central* is the exploration of the moral codes these complex, flawed characters devise.

Europe Central was published after four volumes of the Seven Dreams sequence appeared in print. While both projects are passionate works of historical fiction, their approach to history and historical fiction is different. For the Seven Dreams series, Vollmann undertakes hairsplitting research on historical events and their textbook-level factual representation, draws on the biographies of real-life characters in order to (re)imagine their interior lives, brings to light the history of the oppressed that was silenced or slighted in official narratives, treats history as a series of causal, emblematic events, and focuses on the past's bearing on the present. As Vollmann puts it, the Seven Dreams series is an attempt at symbolic history. In *Europe Central* by contrast, Vollmann does not stick to historical fact as religiously because his aim is to extract moral lessons from the past rather than offer accurate representation of events. He treats the past as material for the parables he wants to write, and he rewrites or modifies facts as fits his purposes. "Most of the characters in this book are real people," he informs us in the appendices; "I researched the details of their lives as carefully as I could. However, this is a work of fiction. Poetic justice has I hope been rendered, both to them and to their historical situations (which got stripped down into parables, then embellished)" (753). If Seven Dreams prioritizes historical events, then *Europe Central* gives primacy to historical figures. For Vollmann, the consciences of individuals who experienced Word World II are what a history of it ought to be built on. In other words, his goal is not to write a history of the war but imagine biographies anew.

The parable format also affects the identity of the narrators in *Europe Central*. Whereas the Seven Dreams novels are narrated by Vollmann's alter ego, William the Blind, *Europe Central* has one identifiable narrator, a Soviet spy who calls himself Comrade Alexandrov, and multiple nameless Soviet and German narrators that tell the stories. As the narrator of the first paired story puts it, "Doesn't the parable possess greater integrity, greater righteousness we might almost say, than any other literary form? For its many conventions weave a holy covenant between the reader, who gets the mystification he craves in a bonbon-sized dose, and the writer, whose absence renders him divine" (14).

Both the Seven Dreams books and *Europe Central* provide scholarly documentation of sources consulted during research, but with a difference. In both projects, primary sources are cited in the appendices. Seven Dreams extends the standard bibliography format and enriches it with chronologies, glossaries, and suggestions for further reading. In *Europe Central,* Vollmann dispensed with the chronology upon the publisher's request, which is surprising because he rarely agrees on cuts. Yet this being an easily accessible timetable of a well-known event from world history, he must have decided that familiarity with the chronology was not indispensable for an appreciation of *Europe Central* (it is the unknown part of the war, made up of stories of the silenced and the morally conflicted, that constitutes a better version of the war for Vollmann). The notes to *Europe Central* mostly serve to identify the sources from which certain remarks, insights, interpretations are derived. Vollmann has inserted direct quotes, translated and retranslated from German, and rephrased original material. Coming across these borrowings, so to speak, at the end of the book, and noticing Vollmann's manipulation of his sources, the reader may get the sense that *Europe Central* is literary montage rather than historical fiction. Alternatively, the reader might see Vollmann as seeking answers in disconnected bits of information, collecting them like a detective and reading meaning into them.

That is exactly what Vollmann's narrator does. Comrade Alexandrov, a Russian spy, opens the novel in 1945, contemplating suicide in a hideout and listening to the telephone whose wires spread over Europe like an octopus and bring him news from all fronts.[4] Structurally, *Europe Central* comprises two parts. The first part contains Comrade Alexandrov's narrative, "Steel in Motion," and the second part contains the meat of the novel in its thirty-six paired stories narrated by various unidentified speakers whose voices intermittently merge with Alexandrov's. The paired stories, usually divided between the USSR and Germany, proceed chronologically and are organized thematically. "Steel in Motion," the single-standing story, may pair well with the book itself. In the wake of the war, Comrade Alexandrov finds that for all his eavesdropping, meaning evades him: what the war was about, or what Europe means, are enigmas to him. He has heard many definitions of Europe while eavesdropping on the phone, but none makes sense: "Europe Central's not a nest of countries at all, but a blank zone of black icons and gold-rimmed clocks whose accidental, endlessly contested territorial divisions can be overwritten as we like" (4). What gives the divisions in Europe any shape, if at all, is the multiplicity of meaning: "Military maps depict them as fronts, trenches, salient and pincer movements. Politicians encode them as borders (*destroyed, razed, utterly smashed*). Administrators imagine that they're roads and rivers. Public health officials see them as black trickles of people dwindling day by day on Leningrad's frozen streets. Poets know them as the veins of Partisan Zoya's martyred body. They're anything. They can do anything" (7). So, what does *Europe Central* imagine Europe to be? As Alexandrov listens to "the shellshocked silence of Europe," the book's hero, Soviet composer Dimitri Shostakovich, closes his ears to what Alexandrov hears and tries to translate Europe into sonatas of love in dedication for the woman he loves, Elena: "Above all Europa is Elena" (808).

Alexandrov may hand over the task of defining Europe to the Soviet composer, but the driving force of "Steel in Motion" and the rest of the book seems to be a brief conversation he has with a Nazi officer on the causes of the war and its carnage: "What set steel in motion? The late SS-Obersturmführer Kurt Gerstein has counseled me to seek the answers in Scripture. . . . He asked himself what he dared not ask his strict father: Why, why all the death? His blood-red Bibles told him why" (9–10). Two former enemies unite in their pursuit of truth, turning to each other for answers. Upon hearing that Kurt Gerstein was killed because he had tried to intervene in the genocide, Comrade Alexandrov decides "to invade the meaning of Europe" (10). Dimitri Shostakovich and Kurt Gerstein are his guides, the two heroes of *Europe Central* who refuse to accept ideology as the essence morality. The questions these characters pose, the questions that *Europe Central* relentlessly pursues, are also the central questions of Vollmann's life: how to fight evil and how to help people?

While Shostakovich appears throughout the book as a major character, a bulk of the narrative being reserved for him, Gerstein features only in the fifty-page story entitled "Clean Hands." Given Vollmann's interest in Nazism, it may come as a surprise that this story is the only direct treatment of the Holocaust in a book of about eight hundred pages. However, since "Clean Hands" embodies most powerfully the paradoxes involved in moral decision making, it is well aligned with the book's purposes.

Gerstein, who came from a family that boasted of pure Aryan blood, is recorded in history for his love-hate relationship with Nazism. In Vollmann's story, his early, enthusiastic relationship with Hitler's party takes a quick downward turn. As a pious man, he publicly denounces what he considers assaults on Christianity, which results in broken teeth, loss of his job, and even imprisonment. Some years later, something breaks him completely and he realizes he can no longer remain a bystander to the crimes his nation commits. He joins the SS with the intention of sabotaging the Holocaust and informing the international community of the crimes Germany is committing against the Jews. "They couldn't have imagined what impelled him: His sister-in-law Berthe had been euthanized at Hadamar. He wished to discover what else was being done in the Führer's name" (417). Although of course he will soon learn that it was Hitler who authorized all the murders, and he will even meet, and work with, the commander in charge of executions of the mentally ill Germans at Hadamar Euthanasia Center. Meanwhile, if Berthe is murdered for being detrimental to the perfection of the Aryan race, Gerstein is immediately admitted as an SS officer because he "received perfect marks for his genealogical chart: one hundred percent Aryan!" (416). The execution methods at Hadamar being identical to those of the concentration camps, Gerstein identifies Berthe with the Jews. Furthermore, he reasons, with brown hair and eyes, "There had been something Jewish-looking about her" (419). The fallacies of racial discrimination overwhelm Gerstein. Confused and angry, he wonders whether he loved Berthe and starts seeing her face in every Jewish woman he encounters. Berthe becomes the face of the murdered but, more importantly, establishes herself as his moral guide. "I am your conscience," she whispers when she overtakes the face of a "dark-haired Polish girl" on a train. "When you walk the dark way, remember me, and always do your best." Gerstein begins walking the dark way, trying to do as Jesus would do in such a situation. "The first time he joined the party, it was out of true German ardor; Berthe was still alive. Then he'd volunteered to be a spy for God" (468).

Berthe's role in this story is crucial. Her death delivers evil to Gerstein's doorstep and enables him to empathize with the victims he had been indoctrinated to hate. She also crystallizes for him the vaguely known but unspoken atrocities committed for the perfection of the Aryan race. She is killed because totalitarianism does not distinguish between the mentally ill and racially other. For Gerstein, all the suffering of the Jews suddenly becomes as meaningless as Berthe's. Fighting against Nazism may seem the obvious and right thing to do but not doing so also seems to be the right thing, for if he were exposed, his wife and children would be in grave danger. But the belief that it is his duty as a Christian to stop the killing ultimately wins out. In a pivotal moment in the story where father and son argue, Gerstein explains that "without practical acts of charity" he cannot fulfill his Christian duty and "choose as Jesus chose" (455, 457). His father's reply is dismissive: "That is perfect fantasy. You're not Jesus. What you imagine is impossible" (457). The real impossibility, perhaps, is managing to hide his true self in an environment completely hostile to it and remaining true to his ideas and values without putting himself and his loved ones in harm's way. This is how Vollmann defines the Pelasgian's dilemma in volume 2 of *Rising Up and Rising Down:* "Do I express who I am, and thereby cause harm to myself (or to those I love), or do I protect myself by becoming one of *them*?" (366, italics original).

In contrast to Gerstein, his father and perhaps more importantly his wife are conspicuously silent about Berthe's death. When Gerstein tells his outspokenly anti-Semitic father that he has proof that Berthe was euthanized, his father offhandedly says she was euthanized legally out of necessity. His wife, Elfriede, on the other hand, remains as silent about Berthe's disappearance as she does about that of the Jewish population. Yet she expects Gerstein to bring home gifts, that is, merchandise and food confiscated from the Jews. Gerstein feels guilty for failing her; "he wondered what the poor thing would have thought of him had she known that he'd turned down all that Jewish butter" (430). When his seniors give him a portion of the gold teeth extracted from murdered Jews, Gerstein thinks he should accept it so that he can sell it and buy food for his family. After the monsignor Gerstein tries to consult with about what to do will not see him, Gerstein in agony asks Elfriede, "What action against Nazism can anyone demand of an ordinary citizen when the representative of Jesus on earth refuses to hear me?" (460–61). When she tells him that "nobody demands of you what you're doing," Gerstein insists, "Our Lord Jesus Christ would have done this and much more" (461). He bravely resists "the allurements of ease, which kept most Germans from doing what Gerstein tried to do," and if we consider his background in theology, the transformation he undergoes may seem striking and perhaps ordinary, or appropriate, at the same time (426). The only friend he confides in likewise implores him to stop going forward. Helmut Hanz is only momentarily shocked over what Gerstein tells him about the concentration camps and warns him: "It's better not to investigate evil things too deeply, Kurt, not only for your safety and ours but also because evil deserves to be respected! Would you strip a leper and expose him? Would you call attention to the ugliness of someone who owns the power to do you harm?" (467). Gerstein's answer is yes and that he is doing it in the name of "our Lord Jesus Christ" (468).

Gerstein's protracted struggle to redefine honor and loyalty as moral concepts drives home the question whether the ends justify the means that is raised by the SS moral code engraved on his dagger: "My honor is my loyalty." He is compelled to accept hypocrisy as his survival mechanism. He is torn between self-preservation and preserving his moral integrity. Should he betray his family and compromise their lives by staying true to his moral code? If he were found out, or if he were to reveal himself, what would happen? He cannot decide how to act but keeps on "trying to learn the contents of more secret documents. This was his honor, you might say" (434). And that has its own consequences, for "how could he deny that with knowledge came sin and death, that his quest to learn the truth had infected him with horror, that he was now an accomplice until he saved the Jews?—But he had clean hands" (435). Vollmann agrees with Gerstein. In the notes to the story, he writes, "I firmly believe that there was nothing ambiguous about Gerstein's good, unavailing though it proved to be. He is one of my heroes" (784). Vollmann gives him Berthe's blessing as well; Gerstein has a hallucination of Berthe on the doorstep of a church. "Do you remember how you told me to go down the dark way?" he asks, and she affirms his innocence: "Look at your hands. . . . They're so soft and white. There's no blood on them" (452). Grateful, Gerstein "kissed her Jewish-looking eyes" (452).

How does the narrator of "Clean Hands" judge Gerstein's efforts to save the Jews and his claim that he is not an accomplice of evil? The narrator cannot locate him in the official histories that think in black and white: Gerstein is not on the "roster of good souls" who risk their lives to help Jews escape, and neither is he on the list of war criminals prosecuted in Nuremberg trials: "Where then is Gerstein? Wherein should he be inscribed?—*Geheim*. His story is rare, and hence as shocking, as full-figure reliefs of the saints on otherwise featureless walls" (424–25).[5] The gray zone in which we can locate Gerstein is described as "falling; he was free to make something of himself between beginning and end" (425). So, whenever he encounters Swedish or British diplomats, bishops and archbishops, he begs them to let the world know about the atrocities of Hitler's gas chambers. Nobody helps him. Nobody helps the Jews. History categorizes him at the opposite ends of the spectrum from hero to villain depending on different conjectures about him. When he is charged with genocide at the end of the war, he writes a letter to his strict father and adds another layer of defeat to his Nazism: "You are wrong about one thing. I never participated in any of this. Whenever I received orders, I not only didn't follow them, but made sure they were disobeyed. For my part, I leave all this with clean hands and a clear conscience" (470). He absolves even the ones who obeyed: "They murdered innocently, because they'd been told to murder and they were stupid. How could Christ himself blame their bloody hands?" (445). In a way, his subconscious seems to reproduce an image that has haunted him from his teenage years, a drawing by communist German painter Käthe Kollwitz that "depicts young, young men with gaping, hypnotized faces marching off all in a row, with a skeleton leading them" (466). Yet he does not consider himself one of them because he recognizes only one leader, Jesus.

Gerstein is repeatedly described as a person disposed to painful self-questioning. "Ever since he was a child, he'd been afflicted by what his father called *evil thoughts,* meaning an introspection of the melancholy, isolating sort. If only he had not had those thoughts! Then he would not have been obliged to cause himself and others so much pain . . ." (426, italics and ellipsis original). For Vollmann, Gerstein's self-doubt when he is doing the morally right thing is one of the most moving aspects of his tale. It is also the most common response to the rise of Hitlerism in Germany among the general population. In his notes to "Clean Hands" Vollmann refers *The Feminine in Fairy Tales* by Marie-Louise von Franz, which helped clarify his thoughts on willing and unwilling complicity with evil: von Franz notes that as Nazism took hold, "'I was several times asked by Germans in what respect they were abnormal, for though they were unable to accept Nazism, not doing so made them doubt their own normality[;] . . . misery fell upon people who had done the right thing'" (784). Berthe, then, may have affirmed a sense of normality for Gerstein, but his misery continues even after he becomes aware of concentration camps and notifies the international community of the secret mass murders in his small, safe ways. It seems to him his complicity with the crimes committed far outweighs the good he tries to accomplish. His job is to make sure that the most effective poison, Zykon B, is delivered to gas chambers: he participates in the Holocaust effectively. The only way to disrupt the killing is to claim that the acid has deteriorated and to argue that the less effective diesel exhaust should be used. "Zykon B suffers from a tendency to spoil," he lies in haste. "In my opinion it's better to resettle fewer Jews per day in a *reliable* fashion than to gamble with an extremely dangerous and uncontrollable toxic agent" (459). After one too many spoils, he falls under the spotlight, and "now he no longer dared to destroy the prussic acid. Therefore he became an accomplice, history said" (460). The irony is that most of the time he tries to make himself look like an accomplice so that he can more effectively intervene. Once, when he was blamed for being "one of those rear echelon assholes who expect other people to get their hands dirty," Gerstein puts on his "healthy fanatical race-hatred," laughed obscenely, and "started kicking the face of a dead Jew" (447). Yet he was not so composed all the time, especially when he was forced to watch gas chambers in operation: "Don't you want to watch the show, Gerstein? We're just about to cram the gas chamber full of naked women!—But they seem so innocent!—Ha, ha! How sly they are!—And his heart screamed out; far away, in Kuibyshev, Shostakovich heard the scream in his nightmares and saved it for Opus 110" (437).

Opus 110 can be seen as the counterpart of Gerstein's logs of Nazi atrocities. If Gerstein writes down the locations of mass graves and the estimated numbers of victims so that the world can one day learn of Nazi secrets, Shostakovich's symphonies register the atrocities of the war from another register. Both men lead double lives, for Shostakovich is forced to join the Communist Party, which he resists, and to advance Stalinism in art, that is, to produce propaganda art. He is under surveillance all the time, his music is subject to tyrannical scrutiny for its noncompliance with program (that is, propaganda) music and for what the authorities deem his "unyielding individualism" (163). Threat, coercion, and censorship are constants in his life. Yet he goes on writing formalist music and resists being dragged into politics. His relatives and supporters disappear slowly—some are killed, some are sent into exile in the hope that this punishment will subdue Shostakovich and his subversive music. An instance of police force in an opera might be read as his "denunciation of police corruption," but what he wishes is "to remind the audience that prisoners are wretches to be pitied, and you shouldn't kick somebody when he's down" (167–68). He keeps his resolve: "If they chop off both my hands, I'll keep writing music with the pen in my teeth," he tells his wife, Nina, who urges him to join the party and surrender his artistic freedom. They keep him alive, however, because he has the talent that can sing of national greatness if he can be subdued. Every time he is harassed, he makes promises he surely will break: "No formalism ever again, he promised. He assured everyone: There can be no music without ideology, comrades! Music is no longer an end in itself, but, how should I say, a vital weapon in the struggle. And I myself, having overcome my, you know, anti-people tendencies . . ." (188). There is a linguistic aporia every time Shostakovich speaks. His sentences run on in a bumbling way and end inconclusively. His self-expression is inhibited, and the loose ends of his sentences show the side effects of the oppression he endures.

Vollmann imagines Shostakovich at work on three major symphonies: the Sonata for Cello and Piano, Opus 40, an ode to his dark-haired mistress, Elena; Symphony no. 7, or the Leningrad Symphony, a commissioned work in praise of Lenin; and the String Quartet no. 8, Opus 110, "the living corpse of music, perfect in its horror" that records the collective suffering of Europe (622). He asks his wife, Nina: "*Can music attack evil?* If I were to try, really sincerely, and perhaps to suffer, and to seek out the sufferings of others, or—"; his words come to another abrupt end (166). He composes Symphony no. 7 under the watchful gaze of the party and its art critics. He tricks them, evades them, and composes as he pleases. Yet "this supposed ode was actually an angry satire against the founder of our Soviet Union. Realizing three or four days before the premiere that this music was practically a death sentence for his entire family, he sat down and wrote a complete new score" (194). Despite these efforts, the symphony is the battle of "two irreconcilable antagonists: Shostakovich's desire to express reality, and his need to please his masters" (215).

Europe Central's longest chapter chronicles the crystallization of Opus 110 in Shostakovich's mind as reality collapses for him. The composer becomes "a mere recording angel," a role Vollmann identifies for himself in the preface to *The Rainbow Stories.* After transmuting into melody the endless march of tanks and artillery explosions and the loud military advance in dramatic brass and cellos, Shostakovich's ears now hear suffering from all over Europe, and he begins collecting every bit of misery for his masterpiece. Musical notation "will scream like invalids in a burning hospital," will choke on "dust which have been smoke from all the millions and millions of burned Jews" (701, 630). As "meaning dissolves into pure music," he vows that he will "make sure that Opus 110 contains *everything,* since it's the last time I'll still be, so to speak, me" (696–97). And he hears, feels, and "becomes every victim" after a lifetime of suffering under coercion to compose music in praise of ideologies that cause such misery (702). He may have remained alive through this ordeal, but upon completing Opus 110, he considers himself artistically and intellectually *liquidated.* He seems to have given up hope in art's potential to fight evil but not in its capacity to represent it. The novel's epigraph is a chilling remark by Shostakovich that confirms his metaphorical death: "The majority of my symphonies are tombstones" (iv).

Vollmann defers to other artists throughout the book and imagines their creative response to war as well. Another figure that records Europe's misery is German painter and sculptor Käthe Kollwitz. We meet her early in the book, in the aftermath of World War I when she senses the impending sequel. "After the World War you'd think that people could have learned something. Naturally, how could they?," she wonders (41). She is as much an empath as Shostakovich is: "Her eyes were not unlike Shostakovich's in that grief seemed almost ready to explode out of them, like corpses flying into the air when a stray shell hits a mass grave" (58). Having lost her son in the war, she paints and sculpts variations of a single image in work after work: woman with dead child, which is both herself and other women during wartime. All her work struggles to represent death. She is an artist Vollmann can easily identify with, for "she found the suffering of others pressed upon her ever more tightly," not imagining but experiencing them herself (38). She resists the ideologically informed artistic movements of her time and "kept painting poor people, starving people (white figures in dark fields, dark chalk on brown Ingres paper), raped women, mothers with dying children. In the end she depicted mainly herself, her stricken, simian face thinking and grieving" (40).

Europe Central owes a lot to the work of Danilo Kiš (1935–89), whose *A Tomb for Boris Davidovich* Vollmann acknowledges in the novel's dedication to Kiš as his companion while he worked on *Europe Central.* How Vollmann came to be a devoted reader of Kiš illuminates his writings' political and historical consciousness. In the summer of 1979, between Deep Springs College and Cornell University, Vollmann discovered Penguin's "Writers from the Other

Europe" series edited by Philip Roth. At that time, he was a bookish, lonely, angry young man who was discouraged by a parochial, commercial U.S. culture that made a virtue out of oblivion and ignorance. Reading the series confirmed his feeling that something was missing from his safe, insulated American life—Tadesz Borowsky, Bruno Schulz, Milan Kundera, Jerzy Andrzejewski, and Danilo Kiš effected, in Vollmann's words, "thrilling and shocking incitements not only to my political development but also to my creative purpose" (*Tomb,* 137). Borowsky's stories inspired his work as a war journalist; Schulz's prose reaffirmed his love for the beautifully crafted sentence; Kiš jolted him awake to the "falsely glamorized" dogma of ideology (139).

Indeed, Kiš shook the ground Vollmann stood on. With *A Tomb for Boris Davidovich* (1978), Kiš transported Vollmann to a new plane of existence and, naturally, to a different literary realm. Kiš's 135-page collection of interlinked stories offers historically accurate parables of communism and anti-Semitism in Europe in the early to mid-twentieth century. In Kiš, Vollmann discovers, first, a model of ideology critique that operates through the ethical force of the aesthetic and, second, the imperative of the literary imagination to rely on the factual. Thus, in his early twenties, Vollmann enters literature's politically and historically conscious space with the awareness that the parable and the documentary are alike in their moral responsibility to truth.

Surprisingly, *A Tomb for Boris Davidovich* is the product of Kiš's effort to find the best discursive form to correct ideological misperceptions among people of Vollmann's age in Europe. In the mid-1970s, while teaching in France, his radical university students called Kiš a fascist and an imperialist because he was critical of Stalin and communism. "These nice young French bourgeois —raised with all the Western freedoms of travel, expression, and access to information," Kiš biographer Mark Thompson notes, "were just as prone to intolerant dogmatism, just as blinkered by ideological prejudice as communists in Yugoslavia. Refusing to accept that his experience granted him any greater insight into communism, they waved away his descriptions of Soviet oppression" (229). Kiš was the son of a Christian mother from Montenegro and a Jewish father from Hungary who died in Auschwitz, baptized so that he could be saved from anti-Semitic hate crimes but self-identified as Jewish, a child of former Yugoslavia under communist terror and ethnic strife, a writer forever oppressed and censored by nationalist hypocrites. If Kiš and his firsthand accounts cannot bear credible witness, what, or who, can? Maybe he embodied a reality too unbelievable to be considered real, he mused; perhaps what was needed for fiction was a believable imaginary. As Thompson puts it, "If the Gulag seemed too fantastic to be real, Kiš should show that the sheer reality of the Gulag was fantastic" (230). He resolved to write fiction based on documented events and persons and to deliver ethnic and political struggle seamlessly within the fabric of mundane life.

At this point, a major yet little known event in the history of world literature took place: as his working model for the task ahead, Kiš turned to Jorge Luis Borges. In the Yugoslavia of the 1970s, Borges "was a cult author" because he "offered an escape from politicized realist conventions" (231–32). However, "For Kiš, Borges provided a means of writing *about* politics" and his "application of Borgesian technique to the Soviet system was a superb invention" (230–33, italics original). He adapted Borges's compact, intertextual stories that make use of "invented bibliographies, quotations from non-existent works" and that ridicule "national conceptions of literature" (230). Like Borges, Kiš also writes minimally and elegantly. He flamboyantly assures the reader of the verifiability of his stories, only to (mis)direct us to nonexistent sources and bibliographies. Moreover, he disdains "any tightly defined concept of national literature. I think of literature as my country of origin," Kiš explains. "I am for Goethe's concept of world literature" (*Homo Poeticus,* 216). Besides Borges, Kiš has affinities with Vladimir Nabokov, Italo Calvino, Bruno Schulz, Joseph Brodsky, Georges Perec, Marcel Proust, and Lautréamont.[6] Of course, in the early nineteenth century, Goethe's idea of *Weltliteratur* advocated the circulation of ideas and works not tethered to the nationalisms across Europe. While our understanding of world literature today expands toward global interconnections, scholars still debate how literature and literary studies can extend beyond national borders. Kiš's derision of nationalism sharpens his worldliness. In "Gingerbread Heart, or Nationalism" he explains that "nationalism—to paraphrase Sartre's observation about anti-Semitism—is a 'free and total choice, a global attitude one adopts not merely to other nations but to people in general, to history and society; it is at once a passion and a conception of the world.' The nationalist is by definition an ignoramus. . . . Nothing 'other' holds any interest for him. Hell is others (other nations, other tribes), people not worth knowing or studying" (*Homo Poeticus,* 16–17). When Vollmann found Kiš, his heart and mind were burdened by his country's celebrated insularity. Kiš instilled in him very early on a desire to know what lies outside and beyond. As a result, everything and everyone "other"—street people in the Tenderloin, cross-dressing women, train hoppers, mujahideen rebels in Afghanistan, Bosnian freedom fighters—comes to hold interest for Vollmann.

If American literary studies feels the urgency of a more globalized literature, Vollmann has long promoted the humanistic principle of involvement on a global scale. Take Vollmann's remarks about the Iraq war in a 2002 speech: "Art is inherently and inescapably political," he reminds the audience, yet "American writers avoid politics (*Expelled from Eden,* 143). In contrast, in

Europe writers are public intellectuals and their thoughts on politics are appreciated. In the absence of a clear picture of the events offered by the government justifying the invasion of Iraq and feeling responsible for an ongoing cultural illiteracy about the affairs of the world among Americans, Vollmann maintains that his task as a writer today is to convey a sense of "how the Iraqis feel about us—in other words, to treat them as round characters" (146). The lesson he learned from Kiš is that the round character is the political and the ethical force of life and fiction alike. He invites his fellow writers and citizens to "treat" the Iraqis "as round characters" to counter stereotyping and promote empathy across cultures and to aid us in seeking an unbiased and accurate understanding of the other's viewpoint (146). "You should get to know them well enough to understand why what they believe is plausible to them," Vollmann says, "and you should explain their views to other Americans as sympathetically and as accurately as you can" (152–53). His afterword to *A Tomb* can be read as the genealogy of his ideas on the importance of round characters.

In his representations of the past, Vollmann turned once more to Kiš, who uses documents, firsthand accounts, research, and his own voice to legitimize the testimony of his texts. Kiš writes self-reflexively about the reliability of his already established sources, and while he seems to make another claim to truth through these assertions, he in fact complicates easy trust in the stated, narrated fact in contrast to the documented fact. Meanwhile, his frequent authorial intrusions offer mostly indirect evidence. Vollmann maximizes these digressions and asides in his sprawling books. Both writers, however, insist on the author's voice as a means of disrupting the homodiegetic fictional world and thereby emphasizing the verifiability of the story and creating the effect of truthful representation. They not only represent recuperated history but convey how history is, and can be, recuperated in the first place: by working within the archive.

The economy of Kiš's prose and the sprawl of Vollmann texts demonstrates how politics can inform the creation and preservation of history. While Kiš reassures the reader that *A Tomb for Boris Davidovich* provides documentation for the unconvinced and the uninformed, no sources or references appear within the book. In contrast, Vollmann's books, especially the Seven Dreams novels of North America's revisionary history of conquest and settlement, abound in bibliographies and glossaries and all other tools of documentation. As Thompson notes, Kiš "reminds us of the Soviet destruction of alternative accounts of history, and the shelf-miles of documents locked away until the USSR disintegrated in 1991" (231). In line with this, Vollmann's encyclopedic rewriting of much of U.S. history may seem to reenact the urge to document every encounter on the new continent and match the immensity of territorial expansion with efforts that parallel the perceived greatness and majesty at hand, albeit with a difference: his is the maximalist novel of America's alternative history that reports the empire to its critics and dissenters and dissects it for its sufferers in rewriting it from their point of view. The professed purpose of Vollmann's revisions is to write fictions that can serve as textbooks in history courses; and he believes his books can do this because he writes, à la Kiš, with his "imagination appropriately filtered and disciplined," which, he maintains, enables his historical fiction to achieve artistic and archival status.

Vollmann's stretch of history weaves America into the fabric of the global world and contributes to "the manifold attempts to change the genealogy of American literary history, to revise beginnings rather than ends" as globalization and the end of "the 'hypernational' era" has called for since the 1980s (Giles, 3, 257). In rewriting history, Vollmann foregrounds the multiplicity and contingency of territorial reconfigurations, giving his work "the potential for opening up new possibilities for the study of America's place within the world" (22). A major part of this achievement is his self-positioning vis-à-vis the world; through reading and writing about literatures of the world and studying their histories, cultures, and politics as much as his own, Vollmann is able to see the planet as an entity with many centers. Any critical effort to understand Vollmann within the worldly context in which he functions must follow Paul Giles in accepting that the purpose of literary studies now "is to bring near and far into juxtaposition, to remap the field according to a logic of parallax so as to elucidate spaces where local, national, and transnational overlap, often in potentially troublesome or even incoherent ways" (266).

Among all the places in the world Vollmann writes about, Central Europe has a special place. *Europe Central* is a direct descendent of *A Tomb for Boris Davidovich* with its focus on war, freedom, and ideology. Both books begin with maps of the locations hosting the interlinked stories that follow. *A Tomb for Boris Davidovich* opens with a bizarre map that renders Europe and Asia a spectral mass. Other than where the land meets the sea, there is no boundary on this map of a blotch for a landform. The only detail fashioning this map-like entity is numbers in tiny fonts that freckle the ethereal landmass like sprinkled sand—numbers that identify the cities and provinces listed alphabetically right below. As we read the stories, boundaries form and reform in and through the hatred, violence, and death that illusory ideology imposes on human life. No single place survives for long; no territory remains on the map forever. Along with people who flit in and out across the interlinked stories, exiting always perforce death, places emerge and retreat in the contingent fashion that defines any territorial demarcation.

In Vollmann's *Europe Central,* the map-epigraph contours Europe and most of Russia. It is a map that is filled up substantially, yet given a map's traditional function, it may be detailed to a fault. While Kiš eschews boundaries in order to amplify their provisionality, Vollmann meticulously traces the claims of different stakeholders on land. Like a transparent palimpsest, this map displays three identifiable layers: the first details in ornate handwriting in black ink the cities where specific military operations were carried out; the second shows military and national symbols signaling the presence and strength of Soviet or Nazi rule; and the third depicts in a grayish fine-tip pen random images of faces, objects, and symbols that leak out toward the blank space of the page—the artist's uncontainable work transgressing territories, boundaries, jurisdictions, warzones. What seems to attract Vollmann to Central Europe is its unique history of nations and borders that can be erased and redrawn by creative minds who give shape to the unendurable mayhem these reconfigurations give rise to through art. As Kiš states in his 1986 essay "Variations on Central European Themes," this is a territory of dissidence, exile, and rootlessness, and it may be a sense of deviation that draws Vollmann to the region. Perhaps the blank map of *A Tomb for Boris Davidovich* alerts Vollmann to the possibility of looking at countries and continents as spaces without centers and margins, to treat borders as nondescript, contingent trifles.

How should we locate the connection between Kiš and Vollmann within world literary history? What precedents would help explain the nature and significance of this literary kinship that is more than a series of inspirations? It is useful to identify precedents because such literary encounters have so far been pivotal models for world literary studies and globalized American literary studies. Wai Chee Dimock and Donald Pease, for example, theorize emergent American world literature through transnational and transtemporal literary encounters. Dimock identifies May 13, 1934, when Russian Jewish poet Osip Mandelstam was arrested and sent into exile in Siberia for his anti-Stalinist work, as the date that announces planetary literature's existence as a "continuum" across territories and chronologies ("Planet," 174). When Mandelstam was arrested, he had a pocket copy of Dante's *Divine Comedy* on his person—a copy that he carried around religiously in the event of his imminent, inevitable arrest. For Dimock, Mandelstam's reading of Dante severs him from "the territorial regime of the nation" and sets off the "global process of extension, elaboration, and randomization" that "turns literature into the collective life of the planet" (178). Six centuries apart, yet "side by side, in defiance of chronology" and properly "denationalized," this literary connection "mak[es] each Italian and not Italian, Russian and not Russian" (176).

Donald Pease further explores literature's thwarting of the state's claim over it in the context of globalism and poses a question: "How can figures from whom the conditions of territorial belonging have been removed, like Osip Mandelstam in the Siberian labor camp, or the detainees in Guantanamo Bay, find a planetary dwelling in which to survive?" (21). Pease proposes June 10, 1952, as the date that marks "the emergence of American literary globalism" (27). That day, C. L. R. James, a literary critic from Trinidad, was interrupted while carrying out research on Herman Melville in the United States on political grounds and sent to Ellis Island, where immigrants are detained for deportation and admittance alike (27). James began writing *Mariners, Renegades, and Castaways: The Story of Herman Melville and the World We Live In* (1953) as he waited to be deported. He interpreted "his political status as a detained refugee" on Ellis Island as something akin to "the narrative fate of the crew" in *Moby-Dick,* thereby connecting and exposing the line between the state's operation and "the interpretive violence Americanist critics directed against the crew" (Pease, 29). If the crew of the *Pequod* is not subjectivized first because Melville feared criticism and then because Cold War criticism reinscribed American exceptionalism, James's writing from the crew's point of view "produced a form of literature for the peoples without literature that could not be included within the extant planetary literary system" (38). In writing into existence the invisible, denationalized, "subnational" status of the crew and of course himself and in recognizing literature's dissent from hegemonic values that encroach the globe, James enacts/performs globalization from below (37).

The summer of 1979 when Vollmann first read *A Tomb for Boris Davidovich* belongs with these breakthrough dates. In line with Dimock's and Pease's analyses, the Kiš-Vollmann encounter becomes a moment in the continuum of world literature not only owing to the status of both authors but also because each introduces variations of extraterritoriality. Possibly the most effectively silenced and desubjectivized entity that this literary encounter delivers for our consideration is geography. Kiš's reading of Pannonia and Vollmann's impression of Imperial that seems to build on the model of Pannonia together offer another transcontinental and transhistorical lineage for literary studies in that they present new ways of extraterritorial living, being, thinking, and writing. Like the Siberian labor camp and Ellis Island, these places are sites of state oppression and subjugation, albeit with a difference: Pannonia and Imperial are imaginary territories that exist only as symbols and dreams that move so far back in time that they evoke their pre-empire phases. They are remnants, erased and forgotten entities. Yet through them emerges the possibility of radical imaginary territorial dwelling and denationalized belonging. Furthermore, they are imagined by people who *feel* extraterritorial without being displaced by authority (though Kiš exiled himself).

Pannonia is "a shorthand for the entire geographical and cultural space" in Eastern Europe that covers today's Croatia, Slovenia, Serbia, and parts of Austria and Hungary (Thompson, 15). Its history begins with water: from a "shallow sea" in the early geological Pliocene epoch, it drains out into a much-desired territory, changing imperial hands among Celts, Romans, Huns, and Charlemagne (15). Pannonia remains a "contact zone" and a migration route for various tribes who identify themselves collectively as "Pannonians" despite the influx of conquerors and their efforts at subduing them (15–16). This is the legacy that informs the symbolic meaning of Pannonia in the twentieth century, when it comes back as an ancient, silent, perfectly subdued yet conceptually overpowering bulwark against ethnic and ideological conflict: "Insulated against politics, it could not be abused or resurrected by nationalists of any stripe" (15). In his "The Return of Pannonia as Imaginary Topos and Space of Homelessness," Guido Snel argues that the very legacy of Pannonia as "a cultural space whose boundaries were more durable than traditional ethnic, national, religious, and ideological ones" allows the imaginary country to stand firm against "nationalist and Marxist discourses" and to propose "in their place an alternative history of continuous destruction, and the homelessness of the individual" (qtd. in Thompson, 17). In his 1972 novel *Hourglass*, Kiš portrays the sediments of Pannonia not as geological strata but layers of human residue heaped on through destruction and the reduction of human life that ideology and nationalism effect (17). Imagining this part of Europe as "a psychogeography" that revives the ethnically, nationally, racially, ideologically irreducible territory of Pannonia, Kiš returns territorial belonging to a preideological state, an "anti-nationalist" stage that stands outside, albeit at the center, of national boundaries and national chronologies (Thompson, 22). Like C. L. R. James in Pease's reading, Kiš subverts and critiques nationalist ideology and its "appearance of orderliness" that relies on censoring or exiling figures like himself by embracing an extraterritorial position (Pease, 42). *Europe Central* gives voice to other artists and dissenters of Central Europe, and *A Tomb for Boris Davidovich*, which sat on Vollmann's desk as he worked on the novel, gave him the moral guidance his characters seek.

CHAPTER 7

Seven Dreams: A Book of North American Landscapes

The Ice-Shirt, The Rifles, The Dying Grass

One day in the late 1980s, Vollmann found himself observing the ugly gray expanse of a parking lot and contemplating the myriad changes that very tract of U.S. land had gone through. What did that particular piece of land look like when it was in the hands of its previous owners and colonizers? What would the knowledge of the transformation of landscape tell us about America? Indeed, what is America? From this fleeting moment of simple reflection sprang an all-devouring curiosity, and Vollmann embarked on one of the most ambitious multivolume historical novel projects of American literature: an ongoing, seven-volume cycle entitled Seven Dreams: A Book of North American Landscapes (1990–2015).[1] For its first colonizers, Vollmann aptly begins with the Norse explorations in ninth and tenth centuries and writes a new origin story for the colonization of the continent. Five novels have so far been published in the series: *The Ice-Shirt: First Dream* (1990), which narrates the Norse encountering Inuit cultures in Vinland; *Fathers and Crows: Second Dream* (1992), which depicts the wars between French Jesuits and the Iroquois from the sixteenth to eighteenth centuries in Canada; *The Rifles: Sixth Dream* (1993), which reimagines Sir John Franklin's ill-fated Arctic expedition as well as the environmental catastrophe that befell the region with the introduction of rifles to Native American populations; *Argall: The True Story of Pocahontas and Captain John Smith; Third Dream* (2001), which is written in Elizabethan English and rewrites the founding of Jamestown in the seventeenth century; and *The Dying Grass: Fifth Dream* (2015), which reinterprets the Plains Indians' struggle for survival in the eighteenth and nineteenth centuries. Vollmann has published the installments without adhering to the chronological sequence: the remaining volumes are *The Poison-Shirt: The Fourth Dream* (covering the seventeenth century, the King Philip War, and the Puritans in Rhode Island) and *The Cloud-Shirt: The Seventh Dream* (covering the twentieth century, the Navajo, and Arizona oil companies).

Vollmann explained in an interview that he took Ovid's *Metamorphoses* as his model for slicing up American history. The Four Ages Ovid envisions, and the idea of decline and destruction with each age, appeal to Vollmann, who likewise envisions American history as an account of gradual degeneration. As an American-history equivalent of Ovid's *Metamorphoses,* this series is a symbolic, mythical, albeit meticulously researched and factual rewriting of the history of North America from the tenth century to the recent past. In this imaginative remapping, Vollmann sketches the continent as a tentative entity that enacts and reenacts the traumas of American history. For Vollmann, American history opens with an episode in a Norse saga that recounts a battle between the colonizers and the natives and continues with restagings of that same kind of encounter. If Ovid attempts "to spin a poem that extends / From the world's first origins down to my own time," Seven Dreams aims at a similarly rigorous and extended genealogy for its subject matter (5). Ovid's frequent borrowing and retelling of myths also resonate with Vollmann's extensive treatment of myth and legends.

Vollmann originally set out to write "a single, seven-part volume that would be this symbolic history of North America over the past thousand years" (Hemmingson, *Critical,* 135). While working on the first part, which turned into *The Ice-Shirt,* the project underwent two major revisions in structure and method. First, because Vollmann realizes compression will be an issue, he expands the projected seven parts into seven volumes and gives each of the seven novels "its own narrative and symbolic focus." Second, he explains, "I began to get more and more interested in being scrupulously accurate in what I was writing about. I decided that if I was going to use the Norse myths, for instance, I wanted to try to make sure to get all the gods and goddesses right, and that all my descriptions of the landscape should be accurately based on my own experience. That, in turn, made it seem only natural for me to get interested in the ethnography and geography of that region so that everything could also be described as accurately as possible" (135–36).

Here we see not only a genealogy of Vollmann's trademark method of research-based writing but also a manifesto for the historical novel that Seven Dreams tries to perfect by way of example, one that emphasizes the novelist's responsibility to assure the reader of the historical accuracy of the story through proper documentation of sources within the space of the book proper. The series expanded in size because Vollmann meticulously records all his research in bibliographies, chronologies, and glossaries at the end of his books, which makes his already thick books even bulkier.[2] His novels, according to him, "straddl[e] the gap between fiction and documentary history" (*The Rifles,* 409), which raises the question of what kind of "history" he deploys as the other of fiction and what he does with it. We may look at the first novel of the Seven Dreams series, *The Ice-Shirt,* for some answers. About two-thirds of the novel relates the history of the first encounter between North America's natives and colonizers by retelling Icelandic sagas and Inuit creation myths. Although the sources Vollmann relies on fashion themselves as biographies and histories, they are fictitious narratives, mixtures of fact and fiction. He privileges tales of demons and monsters and shape-shifting warriors for the versions he supplies of Norse and Inuit history. In a sense, Vollmann considers the fantastic, the supernatural character of these texts as the foundation of something like national character, which he presents as parable, as truth. Indeed, *The Ice-Shirt* opens American history with an axe fable that Vollmann excavates from a battle episode in one of the Icelandic sagas. The Inuit witness for the first time the deadly potential of the iron axe; they leave the battleground and run without looking back toward the forest. Vollmann acknowledges the varying accounts of the same tale in other sagas, but the question, as he puts it in his preface to *The Ice-Shirt* and to all other volumes in the series, is whether "history has a purpose," because "if not, then there is nothing wrong with inventing one" (xxii). Vollmann presents the Seven Dreams series as "an account of origins and metamorphoses which is often untrue based on the literal facts as we know them, but whose untruths further a deeper sense of truth" (397).

The main text of each book in the series is also preceded by an introductory note, an *Ansatzpunkt,* and followed by a section titled "Further Histories." For Vollmann, the function of "these two bookends for the text proper" is to show the reader how the past bears on today: "All these things haven't yet disappeared once the book is over—they still have their impact in the world today" (Hemmingson, *Critical,* 143–44). While the "Further Histories" sections give an account of what happens later to some characters or detail how some events described in the main text evolve and how they bear on the present, they resist resolutions and conclusions. This resolute aversion to closure, noted at times unfavorably by critics, helps Vollmann to highlight the recurring patterns of history and myth in each novel.

Vollmann selects the subject matter of each book in the series by identifying the most representative and symbolic episode among myriad encounters between European colonizers and Native American inhabitants of the continent.

The defining criterion for most representative is "contact or communion or union" between two cultures, because, in his words, if the parties "are somehow intimate with each other, you're more likely to clearly see the effect the two cultures are going to have on each other" (138). Love affairs between Native American women and British explorers or a trusting relationship between a U.S. general and an Indian chief also prove to be "emblematic of American history and the propaganda that's been used to propagate our own image of this history" (138).

While Vollmann seems to redefine the scope and meaning of America in his revisionary history of the entire North American continent, it may strike one as very American to be so invested in space or so interested in locality as a site of meaning, a source of national identity and value. As Paul Giles puts it, "saturat[ion] in locality" is an impulse "to understand that locality as a guarantee of its own authenticity" (11). But Vollmann does not seek such confirmation. He sidesteps exceptionalist dogmas and does not reinscribe locality as the site of a timeless, teleological source of American identity. He offers perhaps a very un-American, dislocating reading of space. It is true that he attempts to understand the character land bestows on a people. But he does not seek a coherent national identity: if anything, he dispels the mystical, mythical readings of America as the new Canaan, a virgin land, and a new Garden of Eden. He writes another story from the standpoint of space, one that multiplies localities, multiplies the meanings of landscape, and ultimately multiplies the spatial and temporal coordinates of national history in an ever-expanding horizon of borders: a reconfigured history of the continent, if you will, and its place within the world.[3]

This is also evident in Vollmann's attempt to recreate his characters' experiences of landscape by experiencing them himself prior to writing. In the small space of a description of the Seven Dreams series addressed to potential publishers, he devotes a long paragraph detailing the places he has visited in order to write the series. Besides multiple locations in North America, from the Magnetic North Pole to Mexico, he also includes Iceland and Greenland as his research destinations. As his plans for travel attest, Vollmann relentlessly seeks the authentic experience landscape bestows without a totalizing impulse. Each site is equally important in understanding the motivations of characters, and seeing landscape as they see it is the foundation of his project.

The Seven Dreams series seems to inscribe American literature into what Wai Chee Dimock calls the "denationalized space" of deep time, the longue durée of world history that eliminates borders and periodizations (*Continents,* 28). Vollmann redefines the adjective "American" as nothing but "a shorthand, a simplified name for a much more complex tangle of relations. Rather than being a discrete entity, it is better seen as a crisscrossing set of pathways, open-ended and ever multiplying, weaving in and out of other geographies, other languages and cultures" (3). If we are to step into deep time, we need to move beyond what Dimock calls "the executive thrust" of such dates as 1620 or 1776 and others that reference landmark events in national history: the attachment to iconic dates merely fosters the idea that America is "a world apart, sufficient unto itself, not burdened by the chronology and geography outside the nation" (2–3). Vollmann's Seven Dreams series guides us toward a wider, more worldly historical context in which to think about American literature, challenging a nation-bound understanding of it. For Vollmann, writing about and defining America is nothing less than extending its circumference in space and time and celebrating the permeability of borders.

Vollmann's "America" emerges out of this long stretch of deep time almost effortlessly. What Vollmann achieves might qualify as anticipating a question Wai Chee Dimock posed in 2001—a decade after the series was born: "What would happen if we were to reckon time by something other than the routine, century-long periods?," Dimock wonders. "What would the world look like if we were to use a different scale, a different temporal taxonomy, a different way of cutting and slicing time?" ("Deep," 758, 755). Vollmann slices history up in a way that disrupts the contours of the nation in space and time and reconceives it as continental entity. Put differently, American history becomes a history of North America in its entirety on the simple premise that history should chronicle beginnings properly. Dispensing with the immigration-colonization-nationhood schema that dates to the seventeenth century, Vollmann avoids deferring to the "executive thrust" of dates. In other words, while each novel in the series identifies a symbolic episode among myriad encounters between Europeans and Native Americans, the episodes do not typically figure in official histories, and Vollmann's slicing up of American history deviates from the accepted reorderings of the nation's past.

The European landfall that initiates Vollmann's history is the arrival of outlawed Icelanders on Greenland in the tenth century. The Norse explorers first encounter and collide with the Micmac Indians in Greenland and then the Inuit in North America when they sail to, as they call it, Vinland. It is not merely because the Norse are the first known colonizers of the continent that Vollmann starts with them: the Norse encounters with the Micmac and the Inuit people help render the otherwise invisible portions of American history not only visible but also foundational. *The Ice-Shirt*, the first novel of the series, is for the most part a retelling of Icelandic sagas, Inuit creation myths, and Micmac legends, a weaving together of the otherwise disparate parts of a shared past. The Seven Dreams series, in Vollmann's words, is neither the chronicle of how the Native Americans were deprived of their land and lives, nor another work in the literature of exploration; it is rather one that replaces a progressive view of history with a regressive one.

There is of course more to say about what Vollmann's retelling of non-American stories and use of non-American sources, whether that be the sagas and myths in *The Ice-Shirt,* or *Jesuit Relations* in *Fathers and Crows*, means for American history. Evidently, Vollmann (re)constructs history as an intertextually rewritten story that stands outside national chronology and geography. This is a kind of revisionary history in the sense that it is a transnational and comparative gesture, one that replaces mythical projections of American space, whether in sacred or secular versions, with another set of reorderings of the literal past. His symbolic reading of the causality between the past and the present proceeds as an infinite number of rehearsals, with the origin point residing outside of official borders and American texts. For Vollmann, anything less would foreshorten the true history—not of the nation but the continent, which ought to be the object of such an endeavor.

The highly visual aspect of such thinking finds a good outlet in Vollmann's reenactment of history through various hand-drawn maps. His cartographic reconstruction of the continent relies on a rethinking of America as a set of provisional maps and fluid borders. Every novel so far published in the series includes maps drawn by Vollmann, which are remarkable in the diverse information they provide: the viewpoints of colonizers and natives are stunningly conveyed and juxtaposed. Moreover, they all rely on Vollmann's own travels and observations. He sometimes contests mapmaking authorities with respect to locations, borders, and so forth. And without these maps—however provisional, or "unreliable" as he puts it—the books would remain incomplete.

We can say that the Seven Dreams series offers at least three definitions of America: it is represented as a "continental" entity that emerges out of deep time, an intertextually, transnationally rewritten story of myths and legends, and a land that reenacts itself infinitely in provisional maps. Reading the spatiotemporal implications of Vollmann's revisionary history with an eye to its radically provisional cartographic imaginary is to read a comparative Americanist text that revises the traditional (exceptionalist) mode of proleptical (re)writing that is common in American literary scholarship (Giles, 255). Vollmann redefines what we mean by "continental U.S.": rather than limiting national space to a certain portion of North America, he expands it toward *and* beyond the continent in time and space. His spatiotemporal reordering of what we might call the national timescape and landscape grants a liberating ungroundedness and uncertainty to the North American terrain, allowing him to reconsider U.S. history and geography within the larger, global framework in novel ways that turn the national "territorializing impulse" to one of transnational dislocation (7).

The Ice-Shirt (1990) launches Vollmann's mammoth history of North America's colonization, establishing the structural standard as well as the thematic focus of the series. Each of the five published installments of the Seven Dreams series concentrates on a singular event and spins a parable out of it by widening the scope associated with that event and including all the moral actors involved. In each case, before the novel proper begins, an authoritative text, or, a historical document on the subject, is offered. These sources illuminate the extent of Vollmann's conflation of history and fiction as well as highlighting the moral lesson Vollmann imparts from those accounts of the past. They function in the manner of the extracts and etymology supplied in *Moby-Dick* and "The Custom House" in *The Scarlet Letter* that precede the novel proper; these are foreword-like sections on their own and essential parts of the narratives that follow. Travel logs and interviews, maps and sketches, glossaries and bibliographies pertaining to the specific encounter documented in each novel also accompany the other books in the series. As the narrator, William the Blind presides over these novels. Despite his steadfast documentation, this is a narrator who revels in being unreliable; he hesitates over and rethinks the facts, discovering the incongruous and irrational aspect of the firmly factual as he composes the book and fictionalizes facts. He seems to uncover only to recompose what Vollmann calls "often untrue based on the literal facts as we know them, but whose untruths further a deeper sense of truth" (397).

In the beginning, there was ice, suggests *The Ice-Shirt*. Starting in an unusual register, the novel commences an origin story through recitations of Icelandic sagas and Indian myths that elaborate cosmogonies of worlds of ice. Although the novel initiates the history of the continent in a realm outside its territorial boundaries and accepted national imaginaries, Vollmann's sources, far from decontextualizing North America, situate the book squarely within the continent's history because these fantastic stories and legends propel the engine of change and establish the theme of shirts that prophesize the shape of conflicts to come and the myriad transformations the continent will undergo. *The Ice-Shirt* paints a picture of a world completely mutable, its order agonizingly impermanent; it not only retells the stories of the magical transformations of the continent but also speaks about the relentless grip of desire and greed on those dwelling on it.

The preamble-like "Ice-Text," whose subtitle reads "*The Book of Flatey 1382*: A Historical Note," sets the stage for this retelling. It begins with a brief introduction to a Greenlandic demon with black hands called Blue-Shirt, or AMORTORTAK, and charts its appearance across Nordic texts. Among them is

The Book of Flatey, a collection of Icelandic sagas, including *The Grænlendiga Saga* (ca. 1190), from which Vollmann draws heavily. What makes this tale special for Vollmann's purposes is its treatment of an event that is singular in its portentousness: during a battle between the Micmac Indians and the Greenlanders around 1000 AD., Micmac warriors get hold of the iron axe, only to discover the effortless death and violence it brings. They take flight from the battleground in horror of such ominous power. This, however, is no ordinary axe; it belongs to Freydis Eiriksdottir, who is "the bastard daughter" of a prominent Icelander, Eirik the Red, and she worships Blue-Shirt like her father. Freydis emerges as the vilest face of human ambition and self-indulgence, a true representative of what Vollmann calls "whirlpool-lives," "devouring and spewing not only those who crossed them, but any in their reach" (48). In the brief span of a couple of pages, the "Ice-Text" heralds three antagonists who figure heavily in the three-year presence of Greenlanders in North America—Freydis, Blue-Shirt, and the iron axe—but before he introduces us to these antagonists Vollmann retells the wonderful myths and legends of Icelanders and Inuit Indians through breathtaking prose, lush descriptions of nature, and astutely imagined characters.

The novel opens with a chapter titled "The Changers: How the Bear-Shirt Was Lost and the Ice-Shirt Was Found" that covers 200–940 AD. In Norway and Sweden, the prehistoric Norse gods Odin, Thor, Heimdal, and Frey rule the earth. Kings of the long-lived Yngling Dynasty carry royal shape-shifting blood. They howl and growl while fangs, claws, and hair grow as they transform from humans into bears. These invincible Bear Kings are "so intoxicated by *metamorphosis*" that they kill and devour on impulse (19, italics original). Yet their "god-blood" thins with the next generations. The Bear-Shirt does not pass on. Around 600 AD, a new breed of warriors seek new glories and begin to pursue "the pale white dream" haunting their sleep, the "immense Ice-Mountain," and move relentlessly westward in search of new lands (34, 40). "They did not know that what they sought was GREENLAND" (40). "Greenland, that stepping-stone to Vinland the Good" enters the narrative like an iceberg looming large on the horizon (44). While the Bear-Shirt gives way to the Ice-Shirt, the "shirt of perpetuity" remains: "Oh, that game of Changing! The players did not really want to be anything; they only wanted to be what they were not. Nobody saw that change came of its own, unfolding as was ordained, so that one would be as ungracious to rush it as to stay it" (19). After the mid-900s, Denmark, Norway, Sweden, Iceland, and Greenland become Christian countries one after another. Greenland soon becomes a reality and never loses its appeal.

Vollmann is at his best in this chapter. He shows complete mastery of the vast corpus of Icelandic sagas in exquisite renderings, giving us a sense of the full complexity and richness of his material. A major part of the chapter narrates the life of Eirik the Red, who is introduced merely as "Freydis's Father" in a section that covers around 945 to 1006 AD (51). Eirik is of noble descent, and his father prophesies that he will pluck "grape-vines" and become great (52). For most of his life, though, Eirik lives the life of an outcast, as feud after feud banishes him first from Norway and then from Iceland, where he takes shelter. Eirik "set sail forever" in search of a place to farm, but "there did not seem to be any place for him" (57, 58). Except for an imaginary place he had heard of from a "wizard and a shape-changer": Greenland (78). Although "the very existence of the country was debatable in those days," Eirik, too, has dreamt of the Ice-Mountain, hence joined "the League of the Ice-Dreamers," and can do nothing but follow the gravitational pull of the mysterious blue mass of ice (74). He sets sail, finds Greenland, and founds a colony that will last for four centuries until the "other Greenlanders," or the Skraelings as the Norse call the Inuit Indians (and all the Indians they encounter), "raided and destroyed the Western Settlement" (78, 81, 82). His children, too, are "destined to reach for new lands" and prosper (65). One of Eirik's three sons, Leif, and his "bastard daughter," Freydis, soon take the stage and American history begins its parable-like unfolding.

Chapter 2, "Black Hands, or, How the Skraelings Put the White-Shirt On," extends the themes of metamorphosis and shirts in retelling the Inuit creation myth and the story of Sun and Moon. The Inuit race has two beginnings. The first is when Elder Brother and Younger Brother come into existence out of nothingness and live on an endless mass of ice. While Elder Brother hunts, the inexperienced Younger Brother is melancholic. He "dream[s] of another brother, who had turned his face from him and gone southward into the ice-mountains, crying out and tearing at himself with his *BLACK HANDS*" (86). He also dreams of shape shifting, whether into a seal, gull, or polar bear. His desire for change is honored by Spirit Woman, whose magic turns him into a woman, and she pronounces the siblings married. She orders the ice to spring up into an island, and Greenland is born. "It was vast and white, and there were no mountains on it" (91). At this point, revealing not only this novel's but also Vollmann's deep interest in various forms of metamorphosis, the narrative makes one of its many atemporal, genre-crossing jumps and moves to San Francisco transvestites in 1987. Under Vollmann's admiring gaze, another boy wills change and turns into a woman, the magic being not so much cosmetics and costumes as the desire for it. No wonder then, in her unending desire to become something else, Younger Brother, now Sister/Wife, takes off her Woman-Shirt and in an excellent imitation of birds dons the Bird-Shirt. She kills Elder Brother before flying away.

When Spirit Woman starts the Inuit race afresh, she gives birth to wolves and dogs. She forbids them to marry their sisters. Yet the desire to transform overwhelms the new race as well: wolves and dogs give birth to humans who quickly become obsessed with shape shifting. In the hands of their shamans, "their ivory-carved ice-bears could come alive; their women's knife-severed fingers fell into the water to become the teeming seals" (103). They call themselves the People, and they thrive on Greenland. "They crossed the ice without fear, brothers and sisters helping each other, never taking sisters" (103). Meanwhile, in another time, in Greenland, Eirik's illegitimate daughter, Freydis, grows up being mistreated by her half brothers, but an "uncanny" ivory-carved seal figure she finds on the pasture gives her fierce spirit the chance to grow (105). "Unlike the Bear-Games in Norway, the Sister-Games were just beginning" (103).

In juxtaposing the curiously similar stories of metamorphoses in Icelandic sagas and Inuit myths, Vollmann merges the Bear-Shirt and the Ice-Shirt with the Woman-Shirt and the Hermaphrodite-Shirt. The story of Sun and Moon also presents a similar case of wayward desire and the perilous change it brings. Sun and Moon are siblings, and until the brother commits incest, they live together peacefully. When Sun identifies her mysterious abuser that comes to her in pitch darkness, she cuts her breast off and throws it at her brother; "As you seem too fond of me, eat me, then!" (109). She runs on the snow holding a burning lamp with blood dripping from her wound and flies to the sky. Moon follows her into the sky. "What is it about the polar heavens that fixes a transient thing for eternity?" asks Vollmann. "Oh, Sun and Moon, how can *we* be happy if you came to be yourselves in this way?" (109, italics original).[4]

How does North America come into being amid these changes? The continent first appears in Chapter 3, "Vinland, or, the Cuttlefish in the Current." At a mere two pages, the chapter seems to mirror the brief presence of Greenlanders in North America. But the chapter also seems to raise the curtain for history's unfolding, now that the rules for the Shirts have been established. Here, Venerate Bjarni, the first Icelander to sight Vinland somewhere between 986 and 995, is introduced. His utter lack of interest in exploring this new land, his peaceful refusal to be a part of this history (and wear the Ice-Shirt), places later explorers squarely within the context of whirlpool-lives. William the Blind, the bard of this saga, says, "I have never yet seen any pictures of Greenlanders in their ice-shirts; so it is now my place to provide one" (128). After an overture of a hundred and thirty pages, the fourth and final chapter narrates the story of the (in)famous "Freydis Eiriksdottir, or, How the Frost Came to Vinland the Good." North America finally arrives in the chilly notes of the *Grænlendiga Saga*.

Leif, the most promising of Eirik's three sons, is ordered by Norway's King Olaf to spread Christianity in Greenland. He "began in Greenland the age of crabbed and ascetic bishops, whose black eyes and black robes would later sweep across Vinland like the wings of crows" (151). While it is debatable how much Freydis can take any religion into her egocentric, icy heart, everyone in the family immediately converts except Eirik. What is important about Leif in this story, however, is not that he carries out Christianization missions but rather the curious thing that happens on his way from Norway to Greenland: his ship drifts in high winds and he accidentally discovers Vinland. "Although King Olaf's priest waxed dangerously anxious, like a mosquito, Leif persuaded him that they would best fulfill their mission to the King by first exploring the new land to see if heathens or Christians lived there" (153). This is a rewarding curiosity, for when Leif returns home with news of "a place without frost" and his lavish cargo of fish, grapes, and timber, he sparks dreams of fortune among Greenlanders, beginning with members of his own family (153). First, his brother Thorvald sails "to win his own fortune in Vinland" (155). He attacks the first Micmac Indians he encounters in Vinland and is killed by them in turn. Yet his men return to Greenland with a delicious load of grapes, mitigating the disaster. It is now the turn of Thorstein, Leif's other brother, to try his luck, but he is half-hearted about the idea. His wife, Gudrid, the daughter of one of Eirik's good friends, teases and taunts Thorstein until she convinces him to sail. Unfortunately, Thorstein dies on the way. Gudrid returns to Greenland and must wait until she remarries for another chance at reaching the edenic land. When Gudrid and her new husband, Karlsefni, decide to go to Vinland, Freydis, wanting to take this "chance to enrich herself," invites herself along (161).

"Freydis was an excellent-looking woman, but her disposition was evil" (163). Keeping the shape-shifting promise of the past alive, she worships demons and magic. In contrast, the equally beautiful, almost angelic Gudrid is a dutiful and resourceful Christian woman. What unites them is their hatred for each other and their dreams of riches. They also inherit life-changing legacies from their fathers. While Gudrid comes into fortune, Eirik bequeaths Freydis the demon AMORTORTAK through childhood bedtime stories, and hence he bequeaths to her his Blue-Shirt and "the great blue glacier" that haunts his dreams. On Eirik's instruction, Freydis sets out for Mount Blauserk, and Vollmann aptly calls Freydis "the evil traveler" on account of her breathtaking, superhuman climb to the glacier (170). She calls on AMORTORTAK when she reaches the peak; the demon answers and agrees to accept her as a servant on the condition that she take ice to Vinland. Impregnated and bonded, Freydis goes to Vinland with ice in her heart and the iron axe in her cargo. Until she fights with the Micmac Indians, at which point the three-year Greenlandic venture ends, she not only trades with them and cheats them in most debased ways but also befriends them to learn their magic and become familiar with their demons for her own advancement.

In this first, albeit brief encounter between Europeans and Inuit and Micmac Indians that Vollmann calls the first age of Vinland, evil knowledge arrives in Eden in the form of the iron axe. *The Ice-Shirt* opens American history with an axe fable that Vollmann draws from a battle episode in Icelandic sagas. *The Book of Flatey* reads, "The fighting commenced, and many of the Skrælings were killed. One man stood tall and handsome among them, and Karselfni reckoned that he must be their Lord. A Skræling had seized [a Greenlander's] axe, and after studying it he swung it at his companion beside him, who fell dead in a twinkling. The tall man then took hold of the axe, scrutinized it, and at last hurled it a great distance out into the fjord. Then the Skrælings fled with all speed into the wood, and so was this happening concluded" (309). Vollmann considers this event "perhaps the most significant in this whole Dream" and saves it for the end of the book, after he has fully developed his idea of human mutability and outlined its early role in North America's history (308). If the Inuit race starts twice, survives, or perishes because of metamorphoses, the axe story suggests what the ultimate refusal of change and the refusal to change looks like: fleeing without looking back for the axe, which is futile because its metamorphosed versions will come back anyway. This encounter, for Vollmann, opens American history because "implicit in the axe is a reified evil which both the Indian leader and the Icelandic saga-writer recognize," and the series "structure[s] its story upon such reifications" (*Expelled from Eden,* 448).

The overarching metamorphosis theme in this novel informs the Seven Dreams series in its entirety. For one, as noted, Vollmann's project is sparked by the urge to discover the transformations the North American landscape has gone through. Vollmann wonders what layers of this palimpsest of a land he can recover meaningfully. This proves to be a daunting and ever expanding task. There is also the fact that Vollmann models his epic after Ovid's *Metamorphoses* and its scheme of the four ages of the human race. Ovid himself borrows this structure from Hesiod's *Works and Days* and enriches it through retellings (Lively, 18). The successive ages of gold, silver, bronze, and iron relate the regression from a state of innocence and peaceful coexistence to a state of greed, immorality, deliberate evil, toil, and immense suffering. The idea of the gradual decline of humankind seems to fit Vollmann's approach to history in his series, in which each of the seven ages of Vinland successively brings more suffering and chaos.

However, it is debatable whether there is any golden age to this iteration of Vinland's history, "The First Age of Vinland," because it seems resolutely anchored in the full horror of the iron age. If ever there was a golden age, it might have been on the immediate arrival of Greenlanders, yet its time is short lived. In Ovid's four ages, eternal spring and an unlimited supply of fruits and grains mark the golden age and gives way to extremes of heat and cold as well as the necessity of hard labor in subsequent ages. The Greenlanders are taken with the sweet breezes and berries of Vinland; they call the land "Wineland the Good," which was "like some treasure of greenness and goodness in the middle of the sea" (321). However, rather than preserving the untouched earth of the Ovidian golden age, the settlers abuse all the generosities of nature, wastefully cutting trees and killing animals. "Not a pine was cut from its native mountain" reads *Metamorphoses,* "to be launched on a maritime tour of the world; / Mortal men knew no shores but their own" (7). Already in the iron age and on alien shores, the Greenlanders soon avert their eyes from the new land and focus on its inhabitants, whom they cheat and kill with their iron axes—a metal they introduce to the continent. It seems that they literally bring the iron age to the continent. Further connections ripe for fuller consideration between the *Metamorphoses* and the Seven Dreams series are that they borrow and enrich myths through retellings, attempt to begin at times of creation and end in the present, demonstrate a preoccupation with transformation as the essence of history and a near obsession with transgression and obscenity, and depict the destruction of unquenchable desire. Last but not least, they are both colossal works made up of a set of stories that nonetheless work toward becoming a single, continuous, unified volume.

Throughout the novel, William the Blind travels in what Vollmann calls in *Fathers and Crows* the "Stream of Time," which signifies, like the "all things flow" mantra of Heraclitus, that we can never step twice in the same river. In transitions and slips in chronology that take the reader by surprise, the narrative goes back and forth in time and observes the specific sites the events take place in and their myriad inhabitants, laying bare the extent of the metamorphoses. These narrative jumps may be seen as both flashbacks and flash forwards in the sense that the past contains the future proleptically or the present forever relives the past, albeit in new forms. According to Robert Caserio, Vollmann is "freely choosing to juxtapose his materials, drawing them from diverse times and discourses, redrawing them at will to shape a discursive in-between 'now'" ("James Cather Vollmann," 174).

The novel's ending is radically open-ended; there is no apparent conclusion to this history's train of change. Freydis cannot bring the ice to North America and returns home defeated. But she is now the one with Black Hands and gives birth "to a lump of ice" (330). From beginning to end, there is only metamorphosis, and no relief from, no reward for, the myriad sufferings it brings.

In conclusion, *The Ice-Shirt* connects the diverging and converging myths and legends of metamorphosis into milestones in the history of North America in order to illuminate the transient moods, characters, and events of that history in unprecedented complexity and resonance.

In *The Rifles* (1994), Vollmann envisions "the sixth age of wine-land" as the age of rifles.[5] This portion of the continent's history begins with the spread of repeating rifles in present-day Arctic Canada in the mid-eighteenth century, a consequence of John Franklin's expeditions to find the Northwest Passage. The explorers trade guns and ammunition for fur, skin, and meat with the Inuit Indians, or, the Esquimaux. Rifles quickly replace the bow and arrow in hunting, and the tribes become addicted to them, for "bullets are media of enslavement as well as currency" (133). What follows is a centuries-long series of ecological crises, gruesome deaths by starvation, dispossession, relocation, and countless tragedies that befall human beings, animals, and nature alike.

If John Franklin initiates the age of rifles, Captain Subzero, one of the two American characters in the novel, connects the past and the present. Yet this is not a smooth temporality where connection between two characters establishes linearity: Subzero, an inhabitant of the 1990s when the novel was written, imagines himself to be the reincarnation of John Franklin. He travels and camps in the Arctic, deliberately exposes himself to the ordeals Franklin and his crew went through, and tries to reenact the historical traumas the novel deals with, playing out a Kierkegaardian mode of repetition with a difference.[6]

To complicate things further, Subzero is Vollmann's alter ego, born while the text is in progress. The conditions necessitating his existence are established very early. Soon after the novel opens, the narrator, who we presume is Vollmann himself, arrives at Pond Inlet in Arctic Canada. He wears a uniform with obscene badges, and no one is friendly toward him. He is a white intruder in a predominantly Native-inhabited place. He comes up with a solution that is morally disturbing within the context of the novel: counting on "the full majesty of the uniform," he begins to introduce himself, dramatically and manipulatively, as Captain Subzero, and begins making friends (29). He believes that being a captain is his "role" (29). The unsettling aspect of Captain Subzero's self-invention is that he comes into being by repeating the native encounter with the alien in uniform, exuding an air of authority. Further, like his forerunners, he too has not come empty-handed: "A canny trader, he had brought chocolate, rubber dinosaur noses, T-shirts and earrings with him from Down South. He won them over by ones and twos" (30). Meanwhile, "many asked Subzero his purpose, and the struggle for absolute accuracy then forced him to be someone he did not want to be" (30). Rather than writing completely from the point of John Franklin, Vollmann deploys Subzero to give him a better understanding of Franklin, a captain. Insofar as Subzero is the fictional counterpart of Vollmann the author/memoirist/traveler/researcher, he is different from other authorial personas of Vollmann. In a metafictional aside, Vollmann writes, "You did not want simply to be someone else in space and time, which was a mere substitution, and, if successfully accomplished, would have left you in an equivalent ontological state; no, you wanted to own alternate selves so that you could be both self and other" (162). Hence the line that introduces the crew of a Franklin expedition: "Franklin, Subzero, you, yours truly, me, myself, and I" (134).

Subzero's controlling presence does not mean that *The Rifles* dispenses with the classic Vollmann trope of the researcher/traveler lyrically narrating facts and experiences. He never disappears from the narrative, whether as an observer or as a metafictional author commenting on the composition of the text. Following the default *The Ice-Shirt* establishes, *The Rifles* begins with a text that positions itself as another log in an Arctic travelogue: "Rifle-Text*:* The Quest for Polar Treasures (1933)." Here we have a traveler taking in the scenery of Resolute Bay. He feels the urge to locate the origin(s) of its exquisite rivers and streams: "You insisted on following your stream to its origin; you were determined to come to someplace definite" (5). We are reminded not only of Franklin's quest to find the Northwest Passage but also his navigational errors, especially in his ill-fated fourth expedition of 1848. Why does such a strong sense of directionlessness and displacement besiege the nameless modern-day traveler? Perhaps he is experiencing how it feels to be lost in an unfriendly territory, an experience the Invit were subjected to when they were relocated here from their home in Inukjuak by the Canadian government in the mid-1950s.

This seems to be the case, as the narrative moves on to an interview with Levi Nungaq, who was among those forced to relocate, separated from family and kin, to a place where his tribe starved because of lack of game and was forced to take shelter against the Arctic winds in canvas tents. Resolute is so windy and uninhabitable that "no bird sang; no sound of life was heard" over there (15). While Nungaq believes Resolute was erected because Canada wanted to claim the region's oil and gas and secure it from Norwegian invasion, others believe the United States "wanted to keep a *friendly* eye on the *friendly* Russian neighbor to the north" (13).

Resolute is more than a setting in *The Rifles;* it is "the capital of Vinland," in that it is the center of lives ruined by evil, a place undone by guns although, Vollmann explains, "Mr. Franklin did not have so much to do with this":

> The French in earlier times had known exactly what they were doing when they introduced firearms into Canada, but by Mr. Franklin's time the rifles

> were spreading faster than smallpox and it was too late to be anything but a dupe; it was merely his weird death that brought us to the Arctic for good, first in the form of search parties, and then as traders, missionaries, police, resettlement administrators, our purpose long and sharp and spiraled like a narwhal horn; and the only reason that Mr. Franklin is germane at all has to do with a certain coincidence of rifles and starvation that I cannot put out of my mind; the whole business is so sad that I do not want to begin, but everywhere you walk there are rifle shells. (123)

It is right that he does not want to begin; one-third of the way into the novel, the narrative still seems to circle around the issues that bother Vollmann. However, from this point on, Vollmann moves on to more focused documentation: a brief history of the development of the repeating rifles in Europe; the aggressive distribution of rifles to the Indian tribes in the Arctic so that they can kill more musk-ox, caribou, and foxes, and sell their skins and furs to the explorers in return for more bullets and guns; vignettes that give statistics on the staggering decrease in animal population, followed by eventual extinction signs by the end of the nineteenth century.

The Rifles brilliantly exposes how in the Arctic hunting is nothing less than overkill—the source of major ecological and ethical crisis. In another authorial aside, Vollmann implores, "My best advice to you, wherever you may be, is to look around you and ask yourself sincerely: Is this continent getting worse?" (132). We cannot answer in the negative if we look at the novel's accounts of hunters killing animals just for the sake of killing in extremely violent, disturbing, and meaningless ways, echoing Natty Bumppo's protests over the staggering number of pigeons killed just because they happen to fly over white men with bullets to spare. Hence, the question of why the novel deals specifically with Resolute, with rifles, and with animals. The problem is "to understand rifles (for you must understand that at this time," Vollmann "was constructing a row of Seven Dreams in order to understand life, and because iron axes had almost decided things in Vinland, because arquebuses had taken command in Kebec, what must rifles have done here?)" (35). In *The Rifles*, Vollmann isolates an element that links his thinking about the ends and means of killing, good versus evil, and the justification of violence in other novels in the series and also in *Rising Up and Rising Down* together: meat.

"Every life contains at least one sadly evil paradox," declares Vollmann, and that seems to inform his approach to animals killed for human consumption in this novel (165). When Franklin is lost and his ship is stuck on ice, and their meat is going poisonous because of lead, he thinks, "We have rifles, you know. There are always the rifles to fall back on" (143). Moreover, "when all else failed there were friendly helpful Esquimaux" (147). Yet their native guide warns them about the risk they are taking: "You proceed far too slowly. You scare the animals away. If you persist, you will all perish" (181). These warnings fall on deaf ears because the English believed "the happy marriage of the rifles and the animals would continue forever, giving birth to meat of the best quality" (183). Moreover, "Mr. Franklin was preoccupied with meat—and who isn't? Duty, love, patriotism and the rest could not exist without meat" (225). But soon, the crew has to resort to eating their leather shoes. Then, they cannibalize their friends and mates. The question Vollmann explores is, what is meat? If it is for survival, how do we differentiate cannibalism from daily meat production and consumption? Can we consider killing a man and an animal for survival on equal terms? What about eating without killing? Subzero's imaginary reenactment of the cannibalism of Franklin's crew deals with this issue. Lost and starving, Subzero stumbles on two dead men on the ground: "He thrust his blade in and began to cut out the heart, hoping to find a little fat. Then he heard the other dead man make a sort of croaking sound and stagger to his feet, glaring and clawing at the air. He turned and waited. The dead man began to walk toward him, chittering. Then he fell and was still forever. Eagerly the one who lived bent over him, made an incision, and drank the hot blood from his throat. He would never have killed another man for food. He would have starved before he did that. But when a man had just died and his blood was fresh, it was a crime to waste it. At once he felt strong and vital again. He cut off some meat and ate until he was satisfied" (319).

Seth, Vollmann/Subzero's American friend and fellow traveler who is wholly opposed to killing animals, is another character through whom Vollmann explores the question of meat, waste, and life. Seth is a botanist. He takes a pragmatist approach to waste and is frustrated by the insulation board in good condition being discarded and a white fox with exquisite fur and a handsome raven that were killed being left behind to rot. He plays a pivotal role in the book's stance on purposeless killing and in the book's depiction of the odd ways that humans try to be good in the face of evil and fail. Seth's failure is that he ends up embracing a reactionary moralism that wavers between a belief in self-sacrifice and a weakness for "fads" (40). "Seth prayed for Raven and Fox in his fashion and wanted to die for or with them" (39). His "sensitivity" and his determination to stand against those who "hurt the world" inspires him to become "a vegetarian to save the rain forest," although Subzero is not persuaded (39). Subzero, by contrast, prefers "making new resolutions on what to be and how to be it, constructing suppositions for why Raven and Fox had been murdered (hygiene? marksmanship? If there was good reason—which is to say practically any reason—then they would not have been murdered after all), wondering about the moral qualities of rifles" (40).

Although there may be problems with opposing Seth's willingness to act to Subzero's inclination for meditation, Seth's point of view is echoed in the novel's all-too-frequent use of epigraphs that document the extent and injustice of the violence toward animals. To the extent that these epigraphs contrast the European approach to hunting and animal life with that of the natives, they function as moral centers of the novel. Fable-like in character, they constitute a collection of vignettes that formulate an ethics of killing and hunting. For instance, the "Rifle-Text" section offers two epigraphs that characterize the real clash between natives and colonizers as one over killing animals with and without a purpose, or killing for food and clothing, on the one hand, and treating animal existence as incidental, subject to human whim and amusement, on the other. In next the section that begins the novel proper we have two more epigraphs, one relating whale hunting as an unprofitable business due to the scarcity of whales, and the other exposing the staggering waste of walruses killed with rifles, as fifteen hundred of the total two thousand killed sink and cannot be retrieved. Whether the animals make themselves available or not, profit and hunting seem to be mutually exclusive. How humans can generate so much waste amid plenty baffles Vollmann, and indeed, the waste is produced as much by humans as by their use of repeating rifles: "Human inertia and stupidity, the two most powerful forces in history (except perhaps for hate) greet us in a bright mirror finish when we turn our attention to the repeaters" (124). Along with *Imperial* and *Carbon Ideologies, The Rifles* is determinedly environmentalist among Vollmann's multiple head-on engagements with nature and ecological problems. The synchronic devastation of fauna and flora, not to mention the concurrent damage to the moral makeup of human beings, is crucial for him.

The novel ends with the starving solo traveler seeing musk-ox and weeping "at the sight of such meat" and thinking "the rifle would save his life" (324). The next sections include documentary accounts of present day Inuit life. There is also a section titled "A Morality Play" that adapts a committee hearing on unlawful aboriginal relocation during which the Canadian government dismisses the grievances of Resolute and Grise Fiord inhabitants at the end of the twentieth century. In the back matter, Vollmann provides detailed glossaries of terms, places, and characters; an exhaustive chronology for the sixth age and a scholarly sources section; a list of gear and materials he used on his Arctic trip; and an acknowledgments section that explains that "Like other Dreams in the series, this book straddles the gap between fiction and documentary history.

I owe a lot to the shade of poor Franklin, a decent inoffensive soul with whom I have taken gross liberties. I owe still more to people I've actually met" (409). And as readers, we owe a lot to Vollmann's hand-drawn maps and sketches that illuminate our chilling way through this novel.

The Dying Grass: A Novel of the Nez Perce War (2015) is the fifth book in the series by chronology and publication order. An exquisite Appaloosa runs across the endless horizon of yellowing grass on the handsome book cover. Although this 1356-page tome breaks Vollmann's personal record in terms of length of a single-volume book, the reading experience makes us feel like we are galloping hypnotically alongside the cover's Appaloosa. Rivers of horses, who murmur "hinimi," accompany the Nez Perces as they roam the Great Plains. A sense of outstretching space is metaphorically and literally at the heart of this novel. Both the Nez Perces and the influx of eastern settlers desire to wander freely across the lush expanse of the land. Meanwhile, Vollmann decompresses the ink-filled portions of the page and rearranges the physical space of the book after the expanding vistas of the Northwest: paragraphs spread out into sentences, and sentences reposition themselves on the page's vast whiteness in expanding and contracting patterns. This novel gives a new shape to the North American landscapes that the series seeks to represent.

Vollmann achieves something incredible with the delicately (and insanely) landscaped form of the book: the unique structure delivers a new form of storytelling. The first chapter opens with a prose poem, then delves into a short profundity that would make modernist masters jealous, and when it comes up for air, it makes its first indent: tabs of line retreat and advance in millimetric depressions, unwinding the perfect heteroglossia of the previous paragraphs toward one of the most innovative typographic layouts in the history of the novel. Each line represents a person's thoughts or remarks in a dialogue. There are no quotation marks to tell us where a dialogue begins and ends or when a monologue or a flashback interrupts a dialogue. Yet each person soon becomes recognizable because of their characteristic manner of speech and dialect, their specific fears and desires, and their particular way of moral reasoning; each becomes a moral actor in his or her own right, shaping their own lives as well as their collective fates. Every formal break with conventional structure and storytelling works toward developing a more realistic, aesthetically uncompromising narrative.

The ebbing and flowing movement of the lines that may at times read like prose poetry or free verse, their careful placement across the page that uses the enveloping white space as the primary means of identifying speakers, conveying their moods, silences, hesitations, and bifurcating thoughts suggests an unlikely influence. Vollmann's closest, albeit paradoxical, kin in this visually empowering novel might be nineteenth-century French symbolist poets, especially Stéphane Mallarmé, who thought of poetry as a spatial and visual form of art and experimented with the typography of the white page by scattering a few words across the page in constellations in such a way that the feelings they evoke rather than their meanings are conveyed.[7] Vollmann, too, treats the whiteness of the page as an aesthetic playground, but his words acquire a direct, plain, realistic meaning against its uncanny muted whiteness. Vollmann does not compress the written word into a fluttering entity on the page. He clears out the page to carve out the space where gritty reality can stand naked, isolated, and be truthfully represented.

In this sense, *The Dying Grass* may be the most visual of Vollmann's books to date. The novel uses this unconventional form in an attempt to capture the workings of the mind and the heart in real time and represent it compellingly. We feel uncomfortably intimate with the myriad characters whose souls are laid out in front of us with complete honesty. We jump from one consciousness to another without losing sense of who is who or the significance of any given moment in the big picture. Even when interior monologues interrupt a character's speech, we can distinguish between his or her public and private personas. As Christopher Coffman puts it, "The indentations force readers to negotiate between layers of action, thought, and speech that subtly interweave the emotions, perceptions, and voices of the many different characters" ("Manifold," n.p.). As far as the physical page is considered, maps, figures, and sketches of plants along with photographs are staples of any Vollmann book. Here, however, the exquisite sketches of endemic plants and flowers that embellish the pages and the eerie photographs seem to give a sense that landscape infiltrates this dream from another register. Beginning with the opening poem's enchanting "and the water / and the grass / and the white ripples on grey water, and white clouds among grey clouds / and the wrinkled young silver skin of the water" and continuing with myriad other descriptions that demonstrate Vollmann's physical immersion in landscape, we are transported into the various mindsets that the same landscape has harbored (13). *The Dying Grass* stands in Vollmann's oeuvre as a mature masterpiece, and it is one of the most exciting, promising contributions to the art of the novel. It is also the Vollmann book that received the most praise right upon publication. However, given the widespread attention this novel has attracted, it remains a mystery why it has not been crowned with literary awards yet.

The Dying Grass chronicles the events of four fateful months in 1877. From June to October, about seven hundred Nez Perce Indians fight with and escape from the U.S. Army in an arduous seventy-five-day, 1321-mile journey across the Northwest (1072).[8] Before the war, the "kidney-shaped blankness" of the huddled Nez Perce land in Wallowa Valley, Oregon, stands as a dreamland in the middle of the Great Plains, provoking the frontier hopes underwritten by manifest destiny (17). Aware that they can no longer stand as an oddity in the tight embrace of U.S. territories around them and survive the influx of American settlers and miners, some "treaty" Nez Perce bands agree to sell their already shrunken land to the U.S. government and move to a reservation. The "nontreaty" bands, however, are given thirty days to move on their own, unless they wish to fight to stay.[9] The peaceful if resigned relocation preparations of these bands (under chiefs Joseph, Ollokot, Toohoolhoolzote, and White Bird) to the unfertile plot, which they call the "Painted Land," gives way to a series of armed conflicts known as the Nez Perce War, as individuals from both sides take matters into their hands.

Besides registering the obvious contexts of post–Civil War U.S. expansionism and the Second Industrial Revolution, Vollmann also filters the Nez Perce War through the lens of the Civil War and its legacies, especially Reconstruction. The novel's sarcastic preamble, "Grass Texts: A Speech and a Report, 1877–78" records the overbearing mood of the previous decade by pinning to the background two events from 1876. The first is the controversial presidential election of 1876, when Republican candidate Rutherford B. Hayes makes an informal last-minute deal with the democratic South known as the Compromise of 1877. He promises to withdraw federal troops from the South and terminate the North's military intervention in the South's domestic affairs and regulations. In return, some southern states fine-tune their ballot results in Hayes's favor. This proves too easy a task: a lapse in military supervision makes it possible to effortlessly—and where necessary, violently—prevent newly enfranchised African Americans from voting. Reconstruction concludes under the shadow of such bizarrely remodeled pre–Civil War conditions. While many differences between the North and the South and between Republicans and Democrats concerning the role of central government and its army are resolved, Jim Crow laws soon dissolve the promises and achievements of the Emancipation Proclamation. At the same time the nation has turned westward for land and prosperity, and Hayes's inaugural address assures the country that "the complete protection of all its citizens in the free enjoyment of all their constitutional rights is now the one subject in our public affairs" (3). The means of such protection hails a cheerful "hurrah for Seven American dreams!" (6).

William the Blind, who is in the Capitol listening to Hayes's speech, exclaims: "LORDY LORD, what could have transpired in our Republic, to render her citizens so unprotected?—Indian troubles, Mexican perils, our vast ocean front, the Silver Panic?" (3). He thinks that "a standing army's un-American" and that government should "let the fools out West take care of themselves. We took care of *our* own Indians" (4).[10] The persona William the Blind momentarily adopts here is crucial: he imagines himself as a Connecticut native and the father of a Union martyr. Apparently, he had become a Democrat after the Civil War but the Compromise of 1877 converts him back to the Grand Old Party. When Hayes mentions "the two distinct races whose peculiar relations to each other have brought upon us the deplorable complications and perplexities which exist in these States," William the Blind protests: "What do we care about that other race? Didn't we bleed enough for them?" (5). What adds insult to his injury is the fact that his son died in one of the major defeats of the Union Army, the Battle of Chancellorsville, while serving in General Howard's unit. "There's the real reason I'm in favor of shrinking the Army," confesses William the Blind: "I want Howard cashiered" (5, 6). Since General Howard, the "Christian General" in whose "hearing you couldn't say a word against niggers" and who later directed the Freedmen's Bureau upon Lincoln's wish and founded and funded Howard University, appears to be "just crazy for darkies," William the Blind insinuates that the Civil War was for naught and so was Reconstruction. "To hell with war-dreams new and old; out with Howard!" (5, 6).

The reference to Walt Whitman's patriotic Civil War poem "Old War-Dreams," where Whitman tries to reconcile his faith in the future of American democracy with the horrors of the recent past, is ironically spot on. "Long have they pass'd," Whitman reminds himself whenever memories of the war's carnage overwhelm him. This evocative line about long-dead soldiers, or the futile effort to convince oneself of the pastness of a malign, spectral past, is repeated throughout *The Dying Grass* to expose the illusions underlying the nineteenth century's optimistic belief in progress, a belief that is blissfully free of any sense of internal conflict and that is not informed by the moral weight of the past. So when Hayes talks about "the permanent pacification of the country," William the Blind protests: "*Long have they pass'd,* so why can't we finally count ourselves permanently pacified?" (4). "*Long have they pass'd;* so let them" (3).

In the second part of "Grass-Texts," William the Blind assumes his usual persona. "Quickly, reader, flitter westward with me," he urges in 1878 from "good old Oregon, where pacification continues its progress"; the nation dreams of "golden-grassed camas prairies out West, so that we can pacify them, permanently" (7, 6). A report dated 1886 unpacks the meaning of pacification. General Howard, the commander of the campaign against the Nez Perce Indians, informs the government that "it will be seen by this report that the Commission failed to settle the difficulties with the non-treaty Nez Perces but made certain definite recommendations" (7). Although General Howard is as devoted to the just treatment of Indians as he was to that of African

Americans during and after the Civil War, during his assignment on the removal of Nez Perces he is torn between his belief in the absolute authority of the government and America's exceptionalist teleology and the conflicting dictates of his conscience. It is ironic that this man who had once dedicated himself to enabling African Americans to own land and subsist on it cannot avoid forcefully removing Indians to uninhabitable, barren grounds. For all the irreconcilable differences between his sense of duty and his moral values, General Howard embodies the dilemmas, aspirations, failures, and accomplishments of the United States in the second half of the nineteenth century. It is possibly his internal strife more than his commanding role in the Nez Perce War that makes him one of the main characters in this novel.

In the sources section Vollmann acknowledges being "haunted" by the discrepancy between Howard's "humane" work with African Americans and his heavy-handed conduct during the Nez Perce campaign (1292). In Vollmann's assessment, the reason "must be that so many Afro-Americans were nominally Christian, while Indians were often to Howard's mind pagans. Their nature-worshipping justifications for refusing to leave their homeland enraged him" (1292). In other words, despite his revolutionary outlook on race, General Howard found himself complicit with enlarging state authority in ways that he both resented and endorsed. The shepherd's maxim, which Vollmann says he follows in *Rising Up and Rising Down,* seems useful here. This maxim posits that "as authority enlarges itself, its obligation to protect from violence the individuals it controls increases, and the ability of those individuals to defend themselves from violence correspondingly decreases" (*Rising,* 662). Within the context of *The Dying Grass* and late nineteenth-century America, violence may have varying imports because as the country expands from shore to shore, so does its authority and the number of people under its jurisdiction, citizens and noncitizens alike. In one reading, to which Hayes resorts, Indian hostility against whites qualifies as the sort of violence that calls for government intervention. In another view, represented in William the Blind's brief stunt, violence amounts to an expression of governmental authority that impinges on individual sovereignty: "When the government calls on you to shed your blood, you've earned the right to speak your mind. And when you're forbidden to call a man *tyrant,* doesn't that make him one? [My son] saw an officer drummed right out of the Army just for disagreeing with the idea of Emancipation. Don't mistake me; I wouldn't oppose it myself; I just don't trouble my appetite about it" (*The Dying Grass*, 5).

The inexpedient, naïve aspect of humanitarianism is at the center of this dream's parable. The main characters, the Nez Perce chief Joseph and General Howard, are both proud not only of their good hearts but also their earnest attitude toward each other. Early in the campaign, they seem to have a mutual understanding of trust and kindness. The Nez Perces, after all, had been the generous and reliable friends of Americans since 1805, when Lewis and Clark met them. Howard first seeks to help the Nez Perces: he wants to "bring them to reason" and move them safely to the reservations so that settlements may begin (96). Likewise, Joseph and other chiefs believe they can talk peacefully, explaining with good cause why they must stay on their ancestral lands. During the so-called peace talks at Lapwai, Chief Toohoolhoolzote tells Howard that they cannot sell their land because they belong to the earth and their "bodies must go back to her" (95). Howard takes this as an affront to the authority of the United States: he arrests Toohoolhoolzote and orders the nontreaty Nez Perce bands to move to the reservation in the allotted thirty-day period. In a previous confrontation, Joseph had smoothed things out by shaking Howard's hand. This time, he "close[es] in upon himself" (95). Soon, however, he appeals to Howard for Toohoolhoolzote's release, calls the assenting Howard "a kind man," and convinces his people to move to the reservation (96). Howard is content: "I have been praying for this result with all my heart . . . I mean only their good" (97). Meanwhile, Joseph is realistic: "They have decided," he tells his people. "We cannot keep them out of our country. Hear me: It is finished" (122). He is also realistic about Howard who "will be killing us all; such is Cut Arm, who pretends to be as kind as a grandfather" (135).[11] The trauma of this episode echoes throughout the novel in refrains: "Thief treaty!"; "Cut Arm showed us the rifle."

Feeling humiliated and betrayed by Howard, the bands convene at Split Rock one last time to meet their relatives before proceeding to the reservation. Although the young ones are stirring with desire for revenge, they respect their chiefs' truce decision. However, the novel's archvillain, Ad Chapman, takes the stage, and things take a horrible, irreversible turn. Chapman has been a welcome white friend of the various Native American tribes for twenty-two years and is now volunteering as a translator in the army. He harbors no evil thoughts toward the Native Americans ("They was fine to me. Treated me right, and all that"), but "they stood between me and my dreams" (784). What he wants is a piece of the Wallowa Valley. So, he takes initiative and fires at the white-flagged Nez Perces, initiating the battle of White Bird Canyon, the first battle of the Nez Perce War, where the army's ambush attempt ends in embarrassing defeat. They claim to have been ambushed themselves to excuse the setback.

At this time, the undermanned and underfunded army is made up of enlisted men who are "the merest runaway thieves and gold-greedy vagabonds" and who do nothing but get drunk and disobey orders (707). The commanding officers are alarmed: "They always get themselves in trouble, then drag us into it. / The General is right. Without them, there wouldn't be any Nez Perce War. / And now we are expected to bleed for them" (370). The volunteering and enlisted citizens' foremost crime may be blaming the Nez Perces for "moral yellowness": they speak continually of their ugly, dirty, greasy, and evil-looking physiques, positing that these men manifest "the outward appearance of evil or violence, the attitude or expression of a human being" (*Rising*, 418). Hence, Doc, the prototypical nineteenth-century explorer of this novel, who comes to the West for riches and to fulfill his dreams of killing the first Indian he lays eyes on but ends up joining the army for the pay and carries on with his usual drinking, causing endless mayhem.

Joseph acts almost like a pacifist during White Bird Canyon and other battles. He is not a war chief and takes no part in the fight that he has warned against and tried to avoid peacefully. His people even mock him for being "chief only of women and children" (*The Dying Grass*, 417). Yet after the first battle, the newspapers dub Joseph "the Red Napoleon," Howard calls him the "mastermind" of the attack, and Chapman screams revenge because Joseph fired first (229). Chapman fabricates lies till the end, and through his outrageous tales, myths build up around Joseph as a rapist and ruthless killer. The unabashedly embellished and obscenely detailed rape and torture of a kidnapped Mrs. Manuel especially consoles the morally conflicted and hesitant hearts or those simply seeking easy justification for ruining the Nez Perces. Howard feels betrayed: "It is strangely difficult to believe there was so much evil in Joseph's heart, but we have now seen his deeds" (229). As the novel progresses, he grows more confident in this false belief and ignores warnings of Chapman's drinking and outright dishonesty. Chapman, however, holds no candle to Howard: "I sure despise that holy fool. If he wasn't a one-armed old melancholic, I'd pound him flatter than Injun pemmican" (899). As Howard's fondness for Chapman grows, we become increasingly puzzled and frustrated at his naiveté, which causes so much direct as well as indirect suffering for the Nez Perces. He tries to be a good person, an understanding father figure to officers and soldiers at his command, and it is both painful and frustrating to see him giving credit and support to every single dishonest and manipulative person around him. What hangs especially heavy in the reader's heart is the surrendered Nez Perces at the end of the war being sent into the reservation with Chapman as their agent.

Another unlikely friendship is between Howard and Lieutenant Wood. If Chapman with his lies and provocations gives Howard a way to justify his merciless pursuit of Nez Perces in battle after battle, Wood serves as his confession booth. Every time Howard fails to convince himself that what he is doing is justified because of Joseph's crimes, he seeks Wood's opinion. Being his inferior in rank, of course, Wood is in no position to honestly criticize Howard. Nonetheless, he cannot hide his sympathy and pity for Howard or his pangs of consciousness regarding the nation's Indian policy, and these expressions of emotion seem to have an effect on Howard. Wood is better at reading character than Howard. He sees, for instance, that Chapman "would like nothing better than a good rape, unless it's to shoot Indians in the back and make money. Out in these Western parts he represents our dominant type: seething, squalid Americanism" (652). Moreover, he seems more down-to-earth in his ethical judgments and self-criticisms. Whereas Howard manages to console himself on the grounds that "we can't stand against Progress, and the way we think about Joseph," Wood feels "immoral in [his] soul": "I comprehend . . . that our cause is *evil,* which is why my hands are more bloodstained than anyone's, even [Major] Gibbon's or Joseph's" (955). Wood is the Whitman of the Nez Perce War; he is a poet, and only he registers the meaning of extreme violence toward dead and alive bodies alike. Especially after witnessing the Nez Perce losses at Big Hole and Bear Paw, where the unarmed elders, women, and children are killed for sport and to facilitate stealing their beads and goods, Wood begins questioning the whole concept of the Indian reservation. Howard assures him it is right, but Wood drifts further away from Howard. If "the real aim of violence is to conquer, direct, instruct, mark, warn, punish, injure, suppress, reduce, destroy or obliterate the consciousness within the body," Wood identifies its operations correctly and takes his stance against it (*Rising,* 150). He resigns from the army and becomes a lawyer.

After the surrender, Howard is sure that he did not "fail Joseph and his Indians" (*The Dying Grass*, 1147). He has served his government. Furthermore, Howard has one last justification: Joseph's "Cayuse blood" (1147). It is "the blood of those who murdered the missionaries. One must never forget that. The rule is as fixed as the stars, that the sins of the fathers shall be visited upon the children unto the third and fourth generations of the men who hate God" (1147–48). Since Joseph refused to convert to Christianity, Howard is reduced to reaffirming his illusions so that he can sustain himself.

The Dying Grass portrays the inner conflicts of many historical characters, and in this respect it is most similar to *Europe Central*. Just as Vollmann does not declare Kurt Gerstein a moral accomplice, so he portrays General Howard and Chief Joseph equally neutrally, letting their weaknesses and strengths speak for themselves. These well-known historical figures become completely new characters in light of Vollmann's exhaustive research; at the same time, Vollmann brings little known or sidelined figures as central as Joseph and Howard into the spotlight. What stays with most readers, though, is Vollmann's extensive use of original Nez Perce names. In the massive glossary of names he has devised to help us navigate the rivers of characters, he includes not only Anglicized version of Native American names and places but also their original spellings, and wherever possible, he offers etymological explanations. Vollmann taught himself some of the Nez Perce language, Nimiputumit, while working on this novel and does his best to recover the Nez Perce as well as other dying Indian languages by deploying original names everywhere possible. Despite its innovative style and intimidating size, *The Dying Grass* is a welcoming, accessible, and gripping book for any first-time reader of Vollmann.

Conclusion

While it does not seem that we are witnessing a radical break between literary epochs, it is evident that an uncategorized, nonunified move has been taking us beyond postmodernism. Trying to identify the defining characteristics of a period we inhabit is a daunting task; there have been a variety of critical attempts, but they concur little on the nature of contemporary American literature's transformations in recent decades. Some are resolute in their belief that the tragedy of September 11 changed the expectations for and nature of literature. In the words of Catherine Morley, after the attacks, "many writers lamented that they had lost impetus, or lost confidence in the power of the pen, in the face of terror, and certainly there seems to have been something of a retreat from the national and the large-scale into the domestic and the local" (106). Some hold that literary realism is once more becoming dominant with the passing of the fashions of experimentalism, nihilism, irony, and cynicism; some see "a renewed wish to return ethical intent to literature after the aestheticizing impulses of modernism and the intellectual abstractions of postmodernism. These writers seek to rehabilitate concepts such as love, communication, and responsibility" (Kelly, 328). Others maintain that the fate of postmodernism is not a relevant starting point for discussing contemporary letters. For instance, in his *The Ecstasy of Influence* (2012), Jonathan Lethem argues that "the reason postmodernism doesn't die is that postmodernism isn't the figure in the black hat standing out in the street squaring off against the earnest and law-abiding 'realist' novel against which it is being opposed. Postmodernism is the street. Postmodernism is the town. It's where we live" (83). In these accounts of contemporary literature a set of writers that includes Dave Eggers, Jonathan Safran Foer, David Foster Wallace, Jonathan Franzen, and in a couple of rare instances, Vollmann (which is odd since Vollmann's body of writing has illustrated many of these concerns long before they found critical expression) emerge as the forerunners of a new sensibility loosely called "post-postmodernism." One reason for the belated interest in Vollmann might be the perceived inaccessibility of his voluminous output, and another could be that the spotlight fell on some of his peers such as David Foster Wallace and Jonathan Franzen, who have been more articulate than Vollmann and many others about the direction of contemporary letters and the problems with literary postmodernism. David Foster Wallace, especially, seemed for a long time to have replaced Pynchon as the unslayable literary father of the so-called post-Pynchon era. It is worth noting that one of his most important prophesies about contemporary American literature in "E Unibus Pluram" reads like an apt description of Vollmann: "The next literary 'rebels' in this country," Wallace argues, "might well emerge as some weird bunch of anti-rebels, born oglers who dare somehow to back away from ironic watching, who have the childish gall actually to endorse and instantiate single entendre principles. Who treat of plain old untrendy human troubles and emotions in U.S. life with reverence and conviction" (81). During their early careers, Vollmann and Wallace were close for a while, and Wallace expressed a mixture of envy of and admiration for Vollmann's rate of production.

Regarding the relentless effort of much contemporary scholarship at periodization, a question Jonathan Arac asks in another context serves as a timely reminder: "We love to write histories that cheer on the emergent and challenge the dominant, but have we yet explored how to write histories of the residual?" (757). Literary critics have identified a number of emergent sensibilities that they argue describe the contemporary scene, yet what is the dominant that the loosely called post-postmodernist sensibility seems to be challenging? Or, for that matter, what is the residual for literary studies at this point? Arac's question may inspire us to push our critical approaches beyond the lines of inquiry thus far proposed for contemporary letters. Two areas of interest seem especially worthy of notice: the so-called ethical turn in literary criticism, a burgeoning area of inquiry that coincides with contemporary fiction's increasing interest in ethics without completely intersecting with its concerns, and the "world-ing" of American literature within the context of globalization.

According to Dorothy Hale, "Since the turn of the new century, there has been an increasing return to ethical inquiry staged by literary critics" (188). Deconstructionists, postmodernists, neohumanists, and moral philosophers have made the study of the novel an integral part of their ethical investigations. But why is it a "return," as Hale, and others, put it? Some argue that ethics has been subject to the "corrosive critique" of postmodern philosophy because it was considered another humanist metanarrative and was theoretically ostracized on account of its naiveté, pious moralism, and superficiality (Voloshin, 69). But when theory allegedly lost impetus around the 1990s, ethics came back in the mode of a backlash. Others maintain that this movement attests to postmodern theory's growing interest in ethics in the wake of the discovery of Paul de Man's anti-Semitic writings and the general concern about deconstruction's neglect of ethics. Perhaps no idea has been more influential in the emergence of postmodern ethics, in part influenced by the deconstructive ethics of Derrida's later writings on responsibility to the other, the gift, hospitality, and forgiveness, than the Levinasian concept of the other and the face.

For moral philosophers such as Cora Diamond and Martha Nussbaum, "the ethical power of fiction" has become more important than "the ethical power of [modern] moral philosophy" (Gibson, 16). For them, "There are 'certain truths about human life' that 'can only be fittingly and accurately stated in the language and forms characteristic of the narrative artist.'" The novelist is a moral thinker who deals with the concrete and the particular rather than the general. However, for a postmodern critic like Andrew Gibson, this is nothing less than a return to "the liberal humanist tradition of novel criticism" in the tradition of F. R. Leavis; the moral philosopher's "sense of the novel and the ethics of fiction is rather prestructuralist" (9). Some literary critics, however, have identified such a return to traditional humanism as a trademark of post-postmodernism.

More important, perhaps, is how formal complexity figures in this discussion. Cora Diamond, for instance, praises Kurt Vonnegut's *Slaughterhouse-Five* (1969) and its "absence of coherent narrative development," irony, and schizophrenic self-definition as signs of its moral vision (49). For her, "the main subject of the novel" is not "how characters deal with morally demanding situations" but how "the features of the text" inform and illuminate its moral thinking (50). Likewise, deconstructionist critic Derek Attridge argues that "the distinctive ethical force of literature inheres not in the fictional world portrayed but in the handling of language whereby that fictional world is brought into being" (653). If we want to read ethically, to do "justice" to what we are reading, we must "atten[d] to linguistic and stylistic details with scrupulous accuracy" (660). For this reason, he privileges modernist writing due to its reluctance to treat language as immediate and transparent (653).

The other helpful line of inquiry in American literary studies has been trying to define new relationships among culture, nation, and world. It has been suggested that "since the turn of the millennium the renewed and intense interest comparative literature in the US has shown in world literature has propelled the discipline to the forefront of literary studies; a large part of this has to do with the reevaluations of America's position in the world after 9/11"

(D'haen, 73). Has the American novel likewise reevaluated its position in the world and widened its horizons? For Bruce Robbins, for instance, the answer is "no." Robbins disagrees with the idea that the American novel has become "worldier" after 9/11. Leerom Medovoi argues that for Robbins, "The post-9/11 novel does a number of things instead: it becomes 'disoriented,' retreats into domesticity, or (at best) treats an outside world of unmitigated suffering and absurdity that justifies immigration in a 'coming to America' narrative. All in all, Robbins finds mistaken the 'gently self-congratulatory' proposition that the American novel has become more global in its perspective, and in that sense more worldly" (643).

So the question is how best to attend to global coordinates in literature. Two recent approaches seem relevant: Gayatri Spivak's notion of planetarity, which she introduces in her 2003 book *Death of a Discipline,* and Wai Chee Dimock's idea of reading the deep time of planetary literature. Spivak calls for "a new comparative literature" that takes the planet as its site of inquiry and dispenses with the terms "globe" and "globalism" on the grounds that these are abstract terms for capitalism that fall short of addressing the desired world-scale reach of alterity. She replaces "global agents" with "planetary subjects" and "global entities" with "planetary creatures" and posits "planetarity" as the default mode of existence and identity, of love and compassion and as the means of embracing the other, which neither postcolonial nor ethnic writing achieve fully at this historical conjecture. Spivak's argument also sheds new light on some recent arguments about what exactly qualifies as "contemporary literature": can either postmodern or experimental works, or realistic, or multicultural writing sweepingly define and characterize the contemporary?[1] Spivak maintains that "we are dealing with heterogeneity on a different scale" and that neither postcolonialism, area studies, nor current practices of comparative literary studies, are able to respond to the alterity of the planet (85).

Wai Chee Dimock's attempt to move literary studies from national to global coordinates by drawing on the idea of planetarity is significant. She privileges "transcontinental ties" of writers across time and space through the notion of "deep time" in which literature becomes a transtemporal "continuum" rather than being confined to the unit of the nation ("Deep Time," 759). Literary kinships that defy territorial and chronological boundaries, that tend toward extraterritoriality, and that suggest more than a series of influences are especially important in this approach, such as the connection between exiled Russian Jewish poet Osip Mandelstam and Dante.

If American literary studies feels the urgency of a more globalized literature in the post-9/11 era and looks for more ethical, engaged writing, William T. Vollmann's works suit the task at hand. Vollmann's interest in the love, empathy, and awareness evident in realms of pain and suffering connects him to other writers. For instance, he praises Nobel Prize winner Heinrich Böll's novella *The Train Was on Time* (1949) on these Dostoevskian grounds. *The Train Was on Time* tells the story of Andreas, a private in Hitler's defeated army. With death close at hand, guilt and regret take over. He suffers, prays, and repents. He repeatedly commits, as Vollmann's 2010 afterword to the novel puts it, "the extreme thoughtcrime of praying for the Jews whom his people are murdering" (130). But it is not just the war that makes him evil. In a scene reminiscent of Vollmann's *Whores for Gloria* or *The Royal Family,* Andreas asks forgiveness for his cruelty toward a hungry and shivering Parisian prostitute. "I wouldn't have treated her so badly if she had been pretty," Andreas admits. "If she had been pretty I might not have been so disgusted by her profession and she wouldn't have been pushed to the gutter" (64). How can Andreas live with himself when death is no longer a vague possibility but inevitably close?

Hours before he dies, he befriends two soldiers. One of them, "the blond one," looks "effete," and his "hideously filmy eyes" betray chlamydia (28, 42). "Maybe he really was effete," Andreas thinks, "but he was a human being" (28). His "disgusting" eyes "didn't stop him offering Andreas bread," nor Andreas accepting the bread (42). The generosity he had refused to the prostitute in Paris is extended to this stranger. For Vollmann, Andreas's "soul has already commenced to grow" in this and other instances of empathy and affection (126). But if anything saves Andreas at all, it is the last few hours of his life in the company of Olina, a Jewish spy in a Polish brothel—his sacred prostitute, if you will. In a scene right out of *Whores for Gloria* where an agonized man hires sex workers to tell him happy childhood stories, Andreas, too, asks nothing of Olina but a conversation.[2] His dreadful certainty about his impending death unsettles Olina, who now begins to regret "sending others to their death" with her spying. That is, soldiers like Andreas. "It's funny that you're a German and I don't hate you," she murmurs, before concluding that his suffering and fear of death is a sign of his innocence (95).

If Andreas is innocent, this probably comforts Olina more than it does Andreas. "Everywhere it's only the innocent who are murdered," Olina concludes. "Everywhere. By us too" (96). She begins to love him in a horrible moment of self-knowledge and recognition of the other. For Vollmann, Olina's belief in Andreas's innocence is pivotal. It is an act of generosity and empathy that can establish a mutual understanding between enemies. Olina embodies "the attempts of human beings, however ignorant, ruined and doomed, to love in whichever way they can, thereby enlarging their sympathies and generosities" (133). Her attempt to save him, however, fails: Olina's escape plan delivers them both to their deaths. The ending of Olina and Andreas haunts Vollmann; his short story "Escape" collected in *Last Stories and Other Stories* recounts the deadly flight attempt and the dying embrace of Bosko Brkić and Admira Ismić, war-torn Sarajevo's Serbian Romeo and Muslim Juliet.

Besides love and empathy, Böll's novella captures Vollmann's other obsessions as well, such as war, death, and the possibility of kindness and affection in unlikely places. Prostitutes, of course, are at the center of all possible analogies. Whereas Andreas follows "this very Catholic notion that pain can be a penance offered up in atonement" and parts with his self-righteous, punitive, scornful heart too late in life, Vollmann's characters that suffer from secular, psychological, existential despair frequently see(k) prostitutes as redeemers, as lovers that can save them (130). In other words, they ascribe to these women what society denies them: the ability to love. If there is anything that distinguishes them, it is their profound understanding of life. As Vollmann explains to Michele Goldberg in an interview, what they have witnessed in life turns any conversation with them into a dialogue with people who have gained sage-like wisdom. However, they do not pretend to be wise or shrewd, because most often they do not fully grasp the true scope and meaning of the evil they encounter. This does not mean that they are immune to malevolence, especially when people are intentionally hostile toward them. Vollmann notes that since he has realized the amount of ill will they endure, he has considered them noble individuals with saint-like dignity.

Vollmann does not consider himself a religious person, but he draws heavily on biblical stories and parables. Prostitutes are the definition of the spiritual in Vollmann's profane belief system. What is deemed carnal, mere lust, is something else for him: Vollmann seems to draw a more honest form of human intimacy and sense of solidarity from his encounters with prostitutes, however temporary their association might be; their endurance and resigned acceptance of immense suffering, their yearning for love and capacity to care dazzles and amazes Vollmann. He goes out of his way to help them—he wants to atone for their suffering. Vollmann here demonstrates a mixture of radical openness to and sympathy and compassion for the other. Like Ishmael, Vollmann envisions a brotherhood that requires nothing less than common creaturely existence. Whoever is deemed fallen by the society, Vollmann considers beatific: the drunk and the stoned show the purest forms of love, compassion, and forgiveness; they endure misery like saints.

Vollmann's approach to women is resolutely carnal and spiritual at the same time. "I have worshipped them and drunk from their mouths; I've studied at their feet. Many have saved me; one or two I've raised up," Vollmann states in "The Shame of It All" (*Expelled from Eden*, 167). What incites cruelty, repulses physically, gives extreme discomfort, and breeds brutal lovelessness is, for Vollmann, the means for living a more generous life. Vollmann assures us that it is possible "to accept the presence of dignity and beauty and most of all *likeness* and *kinship* in something which is ugly" (McCaffery "A Conversation," 16). In his view, only art can achieve that, because only art enables empathy.

While Vollmann rightfully defends the novelist's artistic freedom to empathize with his characters, no matter how evil and morally wrong, the depictions of such characters as the Zombie, the mass murderer in his short story "The Blue Yonder" may lead readers to wonder how much of this empathy is entangled with sympathy or identification. Vollmann says that instead of choosing to remain "righteous and pure" and assuming the morally higher ground, he tries to get into the heads of the evil characters as much as he does the good ones (McCaffery "A Conversation," 17). Imagining the brutality and wickedness of bad people's motivations, moral systems, justifications in all their complexity and horrendousness becomes his task. In line with this, Vollmann's war correspondence and political statements emphasize the importance of bringing imagined (or real-life) characters to life through the novelistic tool of round characters. The context in which he makes that argument is crucial: he talks about people of Muslim faith in general and Muslim extremists in particular, who appear as the ultimate other in Vollmann's writing.

On par with the attempt of the Seven Dreams series to trace collisions between the Europeans and North American natives, Vollmann explores the interactions and confrontations between the United States and the Muslim world. Since his rather naïve decision to go to Afghanistan to join the mujahideen against the Soviet invasion in the mid-1980s, he has continued to pay attention to the Muslim world, visiting Somalia in 1994, Iraq in 1998, Yemen in 2002, and, for a second time, Afghanistan in 2000. Long before the September 11 attacks, Vollmann was already concerned about U.S. foreign policy and how Americans and Muslims categorized each other in dangerously ignorant and prejudiced ways. The average American citizen's response to the attacks as "literal bolts from the blue" and the confusion about "WHY THEY HATE US" trouble Vollmann (*Rising*, 640). His motto is "Find out what your country is doing. Find out what your country has done" (*Expelled from Eden*, 142). He is equally troubled by how Muslim extremists divide the world into followers of Islam and not and apply what Vollmann calls Trotsky's maxim: "No one who disagrees with me is allowed to judge me" (*Rising*, 643). His solution is "build an empathetic bridge between us and them"; "should the bridge remain unbuilt, we must either expect more attacks, or we must eternally police and obliterate" (641). Although Vollmann has provided valuable insights into these issues in his nonfiction, he has not yet built a bridge between these two worlds in fiction.

In conclusion, it is possible to say that in form and spirit, Vollmann operates within the extraordinary. He continuously thwarts our temporal and spatial certainties by carrying us across the planet's multiple zones of existence both past and present and registers a diversity of voices and discourses that makes us hear what the subjugated, the unrecognized, the weak, and the marginalized have to say. This commitment to heterogeneity can be seen as Vollmann's trademark. He leaves the safe space of middle-class conflicts and turns to the unfamiliar life at the periphery. For him, it is the marginal, the loser, the criminal, the victim, and the foreigner who deserves to be written about. Homeless people, legal and illegal immigrants, sex workers, the displaced, and oppressed and exploited people from all walks of life and around the world populate his works. It is his responsibility, as he himself puts it, as a world citizen, a journalist, and a novelist to recognize the other beyond all ideological and moral rifts.

Vollmann's body of writing manifests a relentless attempt to answer what it means to be a human being. Both in nonfiction and fiction, he demonstrates that we are human to the extent that we care deeply about serious and urgent matters and think hard about them. He writes with—and about—feeling, emotion, compassion, and genuine ethical interest in the important realities of human life in all its forms. Vollmann encourages readers to be ethical, too. He invites us, in fact compels us, to treat ethical reflection as our default mode of existence and means of understanding life. Taking stock of Vollmann's intellectual and ethical endeavors across his fiction and nonfiction makes us better human beings because once we observe the true potential of the human in Vollmann, we may revitalize our belief in the moral progress of mankind. Vollmann connects the human to the human and to the world, composing perhaps "saintly books" that bring "word-light" (*Expelled from Eden,* 329). The task of literature as Vollmann described it in the 1990s still holds true: "It is a commonplace that our United States are in decline. On the part of our government we have at best a shortsighted reactive strategy to specific events, lacking in any vision which might influence basic causes. As for the governed, our apathy and misinformation grow hourly. The terrifying increase in random violence and racism of all colors bespeaks a nation polarized halfway to impotence. From homelessness to schools where nothing is taught, from impending environmental disaster to continued environmental assault, our failures illuminate us as Selves incapable of comprehending others" (329–30).

Lacking in empathy, humanity is failing in Vollmann's account, and he makes a convincing case for the essential connectedness of human empathy and politics. In his opinion, literature is "writing with a sense of purpose," and this is the only way to fight against "the woes of the world" (329, 331). In a list of rules, Vollmann explains the goals of literature, crystallizing for readers and critics of contemporary literature the desired contours of any change in literary sensibility:

1. We should never write without feeling.
2. Unless we are much more interesting than we imagine we are, we should strive to feel not only about Self, but also about Other. *Not* the vacuum so often between Self and Other. *Not* the unworthiness of the Other. *Not* the Other as a negation or eclipse of Self. Not even about the Other as exclusive of Self, because that is but a trickster-egoist's way of worshipping Self secretly. We must treat Self and Other as equal partners.
3. We should portray important human problems.
4. We should seek solutions to those problems. Whether or not we find them, the seeking will deepen the portrait.
5. We should know our subject, treating it with the respect with which Self must treat Other. We should know it in all senses, until our eyes are bleary from seeing it, our ears ring from listening to it.
6. We should believe that truth exists.
7. *We should aim to benefit others in addition to ourselves.* (332)

NOTES

Chapter 1—Understanding William T. Vollmann

1. See Michele L. Hardesty's "Looking for the Good Fight" for an analysis of Vollmann's motivations on this trip.

2. In a letter to his editor at Viking, Paul Slovak, who recommended Vollmann cut one-third of his 778-page novel *The Royal Family*, Vollmann calls himself "a bleeding-hearted un-deleter and potential Nobel Prize winner" (*Expelled from Eden,* 319). Vollmann agreed to a cut in his royalties so that the novel could be published uncut.

3. Of course, much of Vollmann's output qualifies as self-reflexive. He draws considerable attention to the fictional status of his writing by laying bare his compositional methods and making authorial intrusions. Such metafictional commonalities, however, do not signal a postmodernist aesthetic. It is possible to describe Vollmann's self-reflexivity as something other than postmodernist playfulness. Maybe this is an example of romantic irony that breaks the illusion of fictionality for the sake of enabling the reader to focus less on plot and more on the narrative aspects of the writing and the workings of language and to emphasize the thoughts and ideas the book should generate, from which follows a sense of his understanding of humanist literature as self-critique and reflexiveness.

4. See Larry McCaffery's introduction to *Expelled from Eden* for an analysis of such claims.

5. It is worth noting that most of his books were accepted by U.K. publishers before they found publishers in the States.

Chapter 2—Early Works

1. Hemmingson posits that books centered on American subcultures "are interconnected in theme, style, and autobiography and form a de facto trilogy. The protagonists—all anti-heroes—are on a quest for human connection, a search for what they consider is love in the guise of a prostitute" (*Critical,* 40).

2. Decades after his visit to Afghanistan, he would acknowledge this effort as naïve at best and an embarrassing failure at worst. However, he still believed that the book itself might help change the course of the war. For this reason, McCaffery considers Vollmann "an old-fashioned humanist who sincerely believes that reading and writing profoundly matter not merely because they supply us with insights and information about the world, but because they can change it" (*Expelled from Eden,* xxx).

3. There are other autobiographical elements in *Butterfly Stories;* Vollmann touches on his being bullied through grade school, his journalistic assignments in Asia, and of course, his frequenting of brothels; in addition, his photographer friend serves as a stand in for his real-life friend Ken Miller.

4. It was published first in the United Kingdom with Kathy Acker's encouragement. Soon after it was published in the States, Vollmann was contacted for a movie production of *Whores for Gloria*. Vollmann adapted the screenplay very quickly, yet the project never materialized.

Chapter 3—*Kissing the Mask, The Book of Dolores*

1. "The woman is more effectively female when tinctured with maleness," Vollmann claims (*Kissing the Mask,* 88).

2. Vollmann notes that the plots of many Noh plays derive from *The Tale of Genji*, one of Vollmann's all-time favorite stories (*Kissing the Mask,* 37).

3. But what is maleness for Vollmann? This question remains unaddressed. For an extensive treatment of this issue, see Lukes, "'Strange Hungers.'"

4. *The Book of Dolores* is excessively technical: Vollmann details the laborious production methods of gum bichromate, silver gelatin photography, block printing, and so forth that he deploys.

Chapter 4—*Poor People, Imperial*

1. Most of these interviews were conducted while Vollmann was working on *Rising Up and Rising Down*. Interview and travel dates range from 1994 to 2005.

2. Vollmann's interest in dire circumstances that affect human moral agency can also be observed in *Into the Forbidden Zone* and *No Immediate Danger* (volume 1 of *Carbon Ideologies*), in which Vollmann wonders why relatively well-off people in both imminent and long-term danger of perishing by the effects of nuclear disasters and climate change seem incapable of understanding their plight.

3. In an essay for the seventy-fifth anniversary of the publication of Agee and Evans's *Let Us Now Praise Famous Men*, David Madden calls the book "the *Moby-Dick* of Nonfiction" (Lofaro, 135).

4. An alternative genealogy for contemporary American literary history emerges as Vollmann updates the concerns of a very specific phase in American literature: he adapts the social critique of a documentary-driven national era to the ethical preoccupations of a globally sensitive transnational period.

5. The example of Agee approaching the underprivileged in such a friendly and sincere manner gave courage to northern civil rights activists working with the disenfranchised in the South in the 1960s. These activists, who called *Let Us Now Praise Famous Men* their bible, were responsible for the revival of this forgotten book from the 1930s (Wolff, 28).

Chapter 5—*Rising Up and Rising Down: Some Thoughts on Violence, Freedom and Urgent Means*

1. Vollmann decided to create an abridged edition because he thought a shorter version could increase the book's chances of being read. Considering that McSweeney's is a nonprofit organization, his choice of the more mainstream Ecco for the abridged edition may seem an odd choice, yet, as Vollmann explains, the justification for the abridgment was financial. This analysis refers to the abridged edition for the convenience of the

general reader. A handful of copies of the seven-volume set can be found on the second-hand market.

Chapter 6—*Europe Central*

1. See Nicholson Baker's *Human Smoke: The Beginnings of World War II, the End of Civilization* (2008) for an unpacking of this myth.

2. "National Book Award Acceptance Speech," www.nationalbook.org/nba2005_f_vollmann.html#.W4Omyc4za70 (accessed July 27, 2016).

3. Vollmann praises Bernard Wolfe's historical novel *The Great Prince Died: A Novel about the Assassination of Trotsky* (1959) for following a similar approach. The novel was reissued in 2015, and Vollmann penned an afterword to it. Wolfe served as Trotsky's secretary before the assassination. His being so highly placed may seem to grant him historian-like authority on his subject matter, yet Wolfe tells us that "this work cannot be called history. It is, rather, a fiction based upon, derived from, dogged by, if you will—history" (401). The word choice is interesting. Is there something stubbornly exerting itself on this novel, we may ask? Is it constraining the narrative? And why such resistance to "history"? We may also ask why Vollmann is interested in this book, for Vollmann is a writer who claims that his own mixtures of fact and fiction are as authoritative as history textbooks, and he has no reservations about taking liberties as a fiction writer and about his departures from chronologies in the service of historical accuracy. *The Great Prince Died* is factual and counterfactual at the same time, presenting itself as both true and false. For one thing, Trotsky is not a character in the novel—despite the title—and his fictional counterpart, Victor Rostov, has at best limited resemblance to him. Among distorted facts are biographical details, such as the number of children he had and the number of times he was married, as well as crucial omissions, such as his role in the violent suppression of the 1921 Kronstadt uprising, and alterations, such as the year he died. What happens between the Kronstadt rebellion and the assassination draws Vollmann to this novel, because, as Vollmann puts it, "*The Great Prince Died* stands or falls by its invocation of Kronstadt" (407). For Vollmann, Trotsky's unspoken, thoroughly concealed complicity in Kronstadt makes him the moral actor of a parable about the ends and means of justifying crimes, including his own assassination, and gives Wolfe the license to depart from chronology so that he can illustrate that point as truthfully and powerfully as possible. Therefore, the novel is implicitly about Trotsky and Kronstadt. Yet if Kronstadt is missing from the novel as a historical event (perhaps to highlight the spectral quality of the "the moment of decision" by "a moral agent"), more than half of Vollmann's eight-page afterword is a "detailed resumé" of this absent center.

4. Alexa̕ndrov is "playing with a Geco, 6.75 shell," which is the gun many disgraced soldiers and officers in the book use to kill themselves (5).

5. *Geheim* means "secret" in German. This word, which recurs throughout the parable, is almost always imprinted on the page to mimic the block-shaped stamp used on government files.

6. Kiš has translated Lautréamont's *Maldoror*—one of Vollmann's favorite books of all time and a self-acknowledged influence on his style.

Chapter 7—Seven Dreams: A Book of North American Landscapes

1. Among similar attempts are John Dos Passos's USA trilogy and Gore Vidal's seven-volume Narratives of Empire (1967–2000) series.

2. For his stubborn refusal to cut these and more from his books and his defenses of the length of his books against editors and publishers, see his correspondence with Paul Slovak and other publishers and editors that are collected in *Expelled from Eden*.

3. See Giles, 1–28.

4. In reference to his sister Julie, Vollmann here asks, "My own true Sun, how long will you bleed?" (109).

5. Vinland, Vine-Land, and Wine-Land are the names various European explorers have given to the continent.

6. Vollmann almost froze to death during this portion of his research.

7. See Mallarmé's *A Roll of the Dice* (1897).

8. Also known as Nez Percé. Following how the Nez Percé pronounce their name, Vollmann uses the unaccented version.

9. The fate that awaited them included the Modoc War (1872–73), the Red River War (1874), Little Big Horn (1876), and the Great Sioux War (1876–77).

10. The army may no longer be the federal guarantor of African Americans' rights, but it continues to be the arbiter of Indian removal campaigns.

11. Howard had lost his arm during the Civil War, in the Fair Oaks battle.

Conclusion

1. See the debate between Amy Hungerford and Gordon Hutner in the 2008 special issue of *American Literary History*.

2. During his research for *Rainbow Stories*, Vollmann, too, hired prostitutes to tell him happy childhood stories.

BIBLIOGRAPHY

Works by William T. Vollmann

FICTION

You Bright and Risen Angels. London: Deutsch, 1987; New York: Athenaeum, 1988; New York: Penguin, 1989.

The Rainbow Stories. London: Deutsch, 1989; New York: Athenaeum, 1989; New York: Penguin, 1991.

The Ice-Shirt. London: Deutsch, 1990; New York: Viking, 1990.

Whores for Gloria. London: Pan Picador, 1991; New York: Pantheon, 1992.

Thirteen Stories and Thirteen Epitaphs. London: Deutsch, 1991; New York: Pantheon, 1991; New York: Grove, 1992.

Fathers and Crows. London: Deutsch, 1992; New York: Viking, 1992; New York: Penguin, 1993.

Butterfly Stories: A Novel. London: Deutsch, 1993; New York: Grove, 1993.

The Rifles. London: Deutsch, 1994; New York: Viking, 1994; New York: Penguin, 1995.

The Royal Family. New York: Viking, 2000.

Argall. New York: Viking, 2001.

Europe Central. New York: Viking, 2005.

Last Stories and Other Stories. New York: Penguin, 2014.

The Dying Grass. New York: Viking, 2015.

NONFICTION

An Afghanistan Picture Show. New York: Farrar, Straus and Giroux, 1992.

The Atlas. New York: Viking, 1996.

Rising Up and Rising Down: Some Thoughts on Violence, Freedom and Urgent Means. Volumes MC, 1–6. San Francisco: McSweeney's Books, 2003.

Expelled from Eden: A William T. Vollmann Reader. Edited by Larry McCaffery and Michael Hemmingson. New York: Thunder's Mouth, 2004.

Rising Up and Rising Down: Some Thoughts on Violence, Freedom and Urgent Means. New York: Ecco, 2004.

Uncentering the Earth: Copernicus and the Revolutions of the Heavenly Spheres. New York: Atlas Books / Norton, 2006.

Poor People. New York: Ecco, 2007.

Riding Toward Everywhere. New York: Ecco, 2008.

Imperial. New York: Viking, 2009.
Kissing the Mask. New York: Ecco, 2010.
Into the Forbidden Zone: A Trip through Hell and High Water in Post-Earthquake Japan. San Francisco: Byliner Books, 2011.
The Book of Dolores. Brooklyn, NY: PowerHouse Books, 2013.
No Immediate Danger. Vol. 1, *Carbon Ideologies.* New York: Viking, 2018.
No Good Alternative. Vol. 2, *Carbon Ideologies.* New York: Viking, 2018.

OTHER SELECTED PUBLICATIONS

"Pornography's Top Components." *Fiction International* 22 (1991): 45–47.
"DeSade's Last Stand." *Esquire,* November 1992, 161–76.
"San Diego, California, U.S.A. (1988)." In *Avant-Pop: Fiction for a Daydream Nation,* edited by Larry McCaffery, 167–71. Normal, IL: Black Ice Books/FC2, 1992.
"Letter from Somalia: Killing Time with the Widowmakers." *Esquire,* May 1993, 63–66.
"Last Days at the Bakery: Sarajevo, Bosnia-Herzogivina (1992)." *Story* (Spring 1994): 42–43.
"Incarnations of the Murderer." In *After Yesterday's Crash: The Avant-Pop Anthology,* edited by Larry McCaffery, 19–29. New York: Penguin, 1995.
"Writing." In *Why I Write: Thoughts on the Practice of Fiction,* edited by Will Blythe, 110–16. Boston: Little, Brown, 1998.
"Letter from Afghanistan: Across the Divide." *New Yorker,* May 15, 2000, 58–73.
"The Best Way to Smoke Crack." In *What the Fuck: The Avant-Porn Anthology,* edited by Michael Hemmingson, 21–33. New York: Soft Skull Press, 2001.
"San Francisco." In *State by State. A Panoramic Portrait of America,* edited by Matt Wieland and Sean Wilsey, 42–55. New York: Ecco, 2006.
"Homeless in Sacramento." *Harper's,* March 2011, 29–46.
"Life as a Terrorist. Uncovering my FBI File." *Harper's,* September 2013, 39–47.
Goldberg, Michele. "Author William Vollmann Shares Vision." *AlterNet.* December 25, 2015. https://www.alternet.org/2000/10/author_william_vollman_shares_vision/.
"Invisible and Insidious. Living at the Edge of Fukushima's Nuclear Disaster." *Harper's,* March 2015, 46–60.
"Letter of Recommendation: *The Gnostic Scriptures,*" *New York Times,* April 11, 2015.
"'I am Here Only for Working.' Conversations with the Petroleum Brotherhood in the UAE." *Harper's,* December 2017, 45–57.

SELECTED BOOK REVIEWS

The Drummer of the Eleventh North, Devonshire Fusiliers, by Guy Davenport. *Philadelphia Inquirer,* December 2, 1990.
Pinocchio in Venice, by Robert Coover. *Philadelphia Inquirer,* January 27, 1991.
Wrong: Stories, by Dennis Cooper. *New York Times Book Review,* April 26, 1992.
Raven's Children, by Richard Adams Carey. *Los Angeles Times Book Review,* July 5, 1992.
American Tabloid, by James Ellroy. *New York Times Book Review,* February 26, 1995.
On the History of Destruction, by W. G. Sebald. *The Believer,* May 2003.
You Alone Are Real to Me: Remembering Rainer Maria Rilke, by Lou Andreas-Salomé. *American Book Review* 24.6 (2003): 24.
Friedrich Nietzsche, by Curtis Cate. *New York Times Book Review,* August 14, 2005.
A Moment in the Sun, by John Sayles. *Bookforum,* June/July 2011.

PREFACES, INTRODUCTIONS, FOREWORDS, AND AFTERWORDS

Afterword to *The Students of Deep Springs College,* by Michael A. Smith, 74–80. Revere, PA: Lodima Press, 2000.

Afterword to *A Tomb for Boris Davidovich,* by Danilo Kiš, 136–45. Translated by Duška Mikić-Mitchell. Normal, IL: Dalkey Archive Press, 2001.

Foreword to *Literotica: The Very Best of Literotica.com,* edited by Lori Selke, 1–5. San Francisco: Black Books, 2001.

Afterword to *Dirty Snow,* by Georges Simenon, 245–57. Translated by Marc Romano and Louise Varèse. New York: New York Review of Books Classics, 2005.

Afterword to *Journey to the End of the Night,* by Louis-Ferdinand Céline, 449–53. Translated by Ralph Manheim. New York: New Directions, 2006.

Afterword to *Under the Volcano,* by Malcolm Lowry, 393–402. New York: Harper Perennial, 2007.

Afterword to *The Train Was on Time,* by Heinrich Böll, 122–33. Translated by Leila Vennewitz. Brooklyn, NY: Melville House, 2011.

Introduction to *The Best American Travel Writing 2012,* edited by William T. Vollmann, xiv–xx. New York: Houghton-Mifflin, 2012.

Afterword to *The Great Prince Died: A Novel about the Assassination of Trotsky,* by Bernard Wolfe, 401–8. Chicago: University of Chicago Press, 2015.

Foreword to *The Saga of Lucien L. Nunn and Deep Springs College*, by L. Jackson Newell, 1–6. Salt Lake City: University of Utah Press, 2015.

Secondary Sources

Agee, James, and Walker Evans. *Let Us Now Praise Famous Men: Three Tenant Families.* 1941. Reprint, New York: Library of America, 2005.

Apter, Emily. *The Translation Zone. A New Comparative Literature.* Princeton, NJ: Princeton University Press, 2011.

Arac, Jonathan. “Literary History in a Global Age.” *New Literary History* 39.3 (2008): 747–60.

Attridge, Derek. “Ethical Modernism: Servants as Others in J. M. Coetzee’s Fiction.” *Poetics Today* 25.4 (2004): 653 71.

Bell, Madison Smartt. “Where an Author Might Be Standing.” *Review of Contemporary Fiction* 13.2 (1993): 39–45.

———. “William T. Vollmann: The Art of Fiction CLXIII.” *Paris Review* 156 (Fall 2000): 256–90.

Brush, Ben. “William T. Vollmann on Writing with Integrity, Bending Genres, and Humanizing the Villains.” *Poets and Writers Magazine,* March 2005, 30.

Bursey, Jeff. “‘A realm forever beyond reach’: Steinbeck and Solzhenitsyn in William Vollmann’s *Expelled from Eden* and *Poor People.*” In *Centering the Margins: Essays and Reviews*, 29–62. London: Zero Books, 2016.

Caserio, Robert. “James, Cather, Vollmann, and the Distinction of Historical Fiction.” *Symploke* 12.1–2 (2004): 106–29. Reprinted in R. M. Berry and Jeffrey R. Di Leo, *Fiction’s Present: Situating Contemporary Narrative Innovation* (New York: SUNY Press, 2007), 159–85.

———. “Last American Stories and Their Adventurous Sequels,” in *American Literature as World Literature,* ed. Jeffrey R. Di Leo, 227–45. New York: Bloomsbury Academic, 2018.

Christiansen, Peter. "Shostakovich in Love: William T. Vollmann's *Europe Central.*" *Journal of the Midwest Modern Language Association* 40.1 (2007): 97–108.

———. "William T. Vollmann's *The Ice-Shirt:* Updating Icelandic Traditions." *Critique: Studies in Contemporary Fiction* 38.1 (1996): 52–57.

Coffman, Christopher K. "Feverish Fictions. William T. Vollmann and American Literary History After Postmodernism." *Textual Practice* 33.2 (2019): 245–62.

———. "Manifold Destiny." *Los Angeles Review of Books,* August 14, 2015.

———. *Rewriting Early America: The Prenational Past in Postmodern Literature.* Bethlehem, PA: Lehigh University Press, 2019.

Coffman, Christopher K., and Daniel Lukes, eds. *William T. Vollmann: A Critical Companion.* Newark: University of Delaware Press, 2015.

D'haen, Theo. *Routledge Concise History of World Literature.* New York: Routledge, 2012.

Diamond, Cora. "Martha Nussbaum and the Need for Novels." In *Renegotiating Ethics in Literature, Philosophy, and Theory,* edited by Jane Adams, Richard Freadman, and David Parker, 39–65. Cambridge: Cambridge University Press, 1998.

Dimock, Wai Chee. "Deep Time: American Literature and World History." *American Literary History* 13.4 (2001): 755–75.

———. "Literature for the Planet." *PMLA* 116.1 (2001): 173–88.

———. *Through Other Continents. American Literature across Deep Time.* Princeton, NJ: Princeton University Press, 2006.

Dushane, Tony. "An Interview with William T. Vollmann." Bookslut.com (November 2005): n.p. www.bookslut.com/features/2005_11_006908.php.

Elliott, Okla. "Wrestling the Octopus: William T. Vollmann's *Imperial* and Biopolitics; or: Rethinking Literary Theory; or: Early Directions in Vollmann Studies." *Southeast Review,* November 15, 2011. http://southeastreview.org/2010/book-review-imperial.html.

Fujii, Hikaru. "The American Traveler's Love and Solitude: *The Atlas,* or William T. Vollmann's Pragmatics of the Double." *Amerikastudien / American Studies* 53.4 (2008): 507–20.

Gibson, Andrew. *Postmodernity, Ethics, and the Novel: From Leavis to Levinas.* London: Routledge, 1999.

Giles, Paul. *Global Remapping of American Literature.* Princeton, NJ: Princeton University Press, 2011.

Green, Jeremy. *Late Postmodernism: American Fiction at the Millennium.* New York: Palgrave Macmillan, 2005.

Hale, Dorothy J. "Fiction as Restriction: Self-Binding in New Ethical Theories of the Novel." *Narrative* 15.2 (2007): 187–206.

Hardesty, Michele L. "Looking for the Good Fight: William T. Vollmann's *An Afghanistan Picture Show.*" *boundary 2* 36.2 (2009): 99–124.

Hemmingson, Michael. *William T. Vollmann: An Annotated Bibliography.* Lanham, MD: Scarecrow Press, 2012.

———. *William T. Vollmann: A Critical Study and Seven Interviews.* Jefferson, NC: McFarland, 2009.

Henry, Casey Michael. "Grooves on the Feeling Knob: Systematic Transgression in William T. Vollmann's *The Rainbow Stories* and Bret Easton Ellis's *American Psycho,*" in *New Media and the Transformation of Postmodern American Literature. From Cage to Connection,* 63–85. London: Bloomsbury Academic, 2019.

Kelly, Adam. "Moments of Decision in Contemporary American Fiction: Roth, Auster, Eugenides." *Critique: Studies in Contemporary Fiction.* 51.4 (2010): 313–32.

Kelly, Robert. "Notes Towards Four Meditations on William T. Vollmann." *Review of Contemporary Fiction* 38.2 (1993): 62–63.

Kiš, Danilo. *Homo Poeticus: Essays and Interviews.* Edited by Susan Sontag. New York: Farrar, Straus, and Giroux, 1995.

———. *A Tomb for Boris Davidovich,* trans. Duška Mikić-Mitchell. Normal, IL: Dalkey Archive Press, 2001.

Lawrence, D. H. *Studies in Classic American Literature.* 1923. Reprint, New York: Penguin, 1977.

LeClair, Tom. "The Prodigious Fictions of Richard Powers, William T. Vollmann, and David Foster Wallace." *Critique: Studies in Contemporary Fiction* 38.1 (1994): 12–37.

Lethem, Jonathan. *The Ecstasy of Influence: Nonfictions, Etc.* New York: Vintage, 2012.

Lively, Genevieve. *Ovid's Metamorphoses: A Reader's Guide.* New York: Continuum, 2011.

Lofaro, Michael, ed. *Agee at 100: Centennial Essays on the Works of James Agee.* Tennessee: University of Tennessee Press, 2012.

Lukes, Daniel. *Conversations with William T. Vollmann.* Jackson: University of Mississippi Press, forthcoming 2020.

———. "An Interview with William T. Vollmann." *While You Were Sleeping* 30 (August/September 2004): 46–49.

———. "'Strange Hungers': William T. Vollmann's Literary Performances of Abject Masculinity," in *William T. Vollmann: A Critical Companion*, ed. Christopher K. Coffman and Daniel Lukes, 247–79. Newark: University of Delaware Press, 2015.

McCaffery, Larry. "A Conversation with William T. Vollmann." *Review of Contemporary Fiction* 13.2 (1993): 9–24.

McLaughlin, Robert L. "Post-Postmodern Discontent: Contemporary Fiction and the Social World." In *Fiction's Present: Situating Contemporary Narrative Innovation,* edited by R. M. Berry and Jeffrey R. Di Leo, 101–19. Albany, NY: State University of New York Press, 2008.

Medovoi, Leerom. "'Terminal Crisis?' From the Worlding of American Literature to World-System Literature." *American Literary History* 23:3 (2011): 643–59.

Mellor, Michael A. T. *William T. Vollmann: Writing America's Other Histories.* Forthcoming.

Morley, Catherine. *The Quest for Epic in Contemporary American Fiction: John Updike, Philip Roth and Don DeLillo.* New York: Routledge, 2009.

Newell, L. Jackson. *The Electric Edge of Academe. The Saga of Lucien L. Nunn and Deep Springs College.* Salt Lake City: University of Utah Press, 2015.

Ovid. *Metamorphoses.* Translated by Stanley Lombardo. Indianapolis, IN: Hackett, 2010.

Palleau-Papin, Françoise. "Uncentering the Self: William T. Vollmann's Copernican System in *The Atlas.*" In *Science and American Literature in the 20th and 21st Centuries: From Henry Adams to John Adams,* edited by Claire Maniez, Ronan Ludot-Vlasak, and Frédéric Dumas, 117–28. Newcastle, U.K.: Cambridge Scholars Publishing, 2012.

———, ed. *Under Fire: William T. Vollmann, The Rifles.* Bern: Peter Lang, 2016.

Pease, Donald. "The Extraterritoriality of the Literature for Our Planet." *ESQ: A Journal of the American Renaissance* 50.1–3 (2004): 177–221.

Rebein, Robert. *Hicks, Tribes, and Dirty Realists: American Fiction after Postmodernism.* Lexington: University Press of Kentucky, 2001.

Ross, Stephen. "A Modest Imperialist: William T. Vollmann." *Brooklyn Rail,* March 4, 2010.

Savvas, Theophilus. *American Postmodernist Fiction and the Past.* London: Palgrave Macmillan, 2011.

Smith, Carlton. "Arctic Revelations: Vollmann's *The Rifles* and the Frozen Landscape of the Self." *Review of Contemporary Fiction* 13.2 (1993): 53–61.

Spivak, Gayatri Chakravorty. *Death of a Discipline.* New York: Columbia University Press. 2003.

Steinbeck, John. *Steinbeck: A Life in Letters.* Edited by Elaine Steinbeck and Robert Wallasten. New York: Penguin, 1989.

Thompson, Mark. *Birth Certificate. The Story of Danilo Kiš.* Ithaca, NY: Cornell University Press, 2013.

Thorne, Matt. "What's in the Meat Locker, Bill?" *Independent* (London), August 6, 2006.

Ulin, David L. "William T. Vollmann: The Dispassionate Chronicler." *Los Angeles Times,* November 1, 2009.

Voloshin, Beverly R. "The Ethical Turn in French Philosophy." *Pacific Coast Philology* 33.1 (1998): 69–86.

Wallace, David Foster. *A Supposedly Fun Thing I'll Never Do Again. Essays and Arguments.* Boston: Back Bay Books, 1998.

Wolff, Daniel. "And the Truth Shall Make You Free." *Threepenny Review* 41 (Spring 1990): 28–29.

INDEX